10⁹⁵/₁₂⁵

Sex and Subterfuge

Sex and Subterfuge

Women Writers to 1850

EVA FIGES

PERSEA BOOKS
New York

First published in Great Britain by The Macmillan Press Ltd. in 1982. First published in the United States in 1988 by Persea Books, 60 Madison Avenue, New York, New York 10010.

Library of Congress Cataloging-in-Publication Data

Figes, Eva.
    Sex & subterfuge.

    Bibliography: p.
    Includes index.
    1. English fiction—Women authors—History and criticism. 2. English fiction—19th century—History and criticism. 3. English fiction—18th century—History and criticism. 4. Women and literature—Great Britain—History—19th century. 5. Women and literature—Great Britain—History—18th century. 6. Women in literature. I. Title. II. Title: Sex and subterfuge.
PR111.F54   1988   823'.009'9287   88-4082
ISBN 0-89255-129-1 (pbk.)

The author wishes to acknowledge the receipt of a Research Award from the Leverhulme Trust to help with expenses incurred during the completion of this book.

Manufactured in the United States.

First printing

Contents

Acknowledgement

The author wishes to acknowledge the receipt of a Research Award from the Leverhulme Trust to help with expenses incurred during the completion of this book.

Introduction

THROUGHOUT the eighteenth century women had been writing popular novels, largely for the consumption of other women, and both production and consumption were viewed with considerable contempt by the superior sex. But during the last decade of the eighteenth century a change took place: women began to write novels with a skill and authority which commanded the respect of both sexes, and over the next fifty years they colonised the medium and made it their own. They took over the novel in England, gave it a new shape, structure and unity of intention which was to have a lasting impact to this day. If there is such a thing as the classical novel in English literature, and I think there is, then women were responsible for defining and refining it.

The novel which women took over from men towards the end of the eighteenth century was a bulky, amorphous affair. Virginia Woolf, in *A Room of One's Own*, expressed the hope that women writers would, in the future, write novels which were rather shorter than those of men. Her own novels are certainly a good deal shorter than those of Joyce, Proust or Mann. But if she had looked at the history of the novel to her own time she would have realised that most women have tended to value brevity. *Evelina*, although an epistolary novel, is much shorter than anything by Richardson; Austen pruned and polished *Pride and Prejudice* for years before she sent it off to a publisher; Charlotte Brontë, making notes for a possible first novel while a student teacher in Brussels, reminded herself to 'Avoid Richardsonian multiplication' and aim for 'As much compression – as little explanation as may be'.[1] On the whole the best of women's fiction tends to be short and compressed, certainly compared with the best output by male writers. George Eliot, writing at the peak of the Victorian era, building on the groundwork done by earlier women writers and competing against male professionalism in a way that Austen or the Brontës or even Mrs Gaskell had never done, did go in for bulk.

But George Eliot's structures were still basically female structures, an elaboration of what the best women writers had done in the sixty or seventy years before she began to write. The typical male structure was inherited from Fielding: it was linear, episodic and picaresque. The hero moved from adventure to adventure, scene to scene, characters popped up and then vanished for an age; often there were tales told by a peripheral character within the main narrative. It is a technique aptly satirised in Sterne's *Tristram Shandy*, where much is said but the hero never even suceeds in getting himself born.

This is the male mode taken over and adapted by Dickens and to some extent by Thackeray. It lends itself to serial publication, particularly when the aim is to get as much financial gain as possible from one storyline, and also to spin it out. 'There are superb passages in it; but what defective composition!' Flaubert wrote to George Sand after reading *Pickwick Papers*, perhaps not a fair example, although Dickens simply developed that early technique. Flaubert goes on to comment: 'All English writers are the same; Walter Scott excepted, all lack a plot. That is unendurable for us Latins.'[2] Not only Walter Scott, but every woman writer between Austen and Eliot must also be excepted.

Bulk in England has tended to be associated with committed professionalism and the need or wish for financial gain. The women who wrote long novels at this period tended to be women who turned to writing as a means of gaining an independent existence, Charlotte Smith, for instance, Mrs Radcliffe, and the later Fanny Burney. Financial considerations were also important to George Eliot once she was established as a novelist and could give up literary hack work. But women writers, the best of them, seem never to have lost sight of the need for aesthetic integrity, the need to see a novel as a whole. While Dickens and Thackeray wrote chapter by chapter to a deadline for serial publication, Charlotte Brontë and George Eliot refused to be published in this way because it was clearly damaging to the idea of the novel as a whole. When Mrs Gaskell was lured into serial publication by Dickens she refused to adapt or compromise in the way serial publication demanded, and cost Dickens many of the readers he had been assiduously wooing with his own work.

It is the intention of this book to examine the literary progress of women novelists during this key period in their emergence from the shadows of obscurity. We are so used to thinking of the 'disadvantages' of women (if we are women) and the 'inferiority' of women (if we are men) that it might come as a surprise to both to find a situation where disadvantages turned out to be advantages and the supposedly inferior sex showed itself to be unexpectedly superior.

1. Background for Change

WHY was it that both the quantity and quality of fiction written by women increased so significantly towards the end of the eighteenth century? To find some of the answers we have to look at the social changes taking place.

Women novelists came from the social classes who could indulge in the luxury of educating their daughters. Maria Edgeworth and Jane Austen were born into the gentry, Fanny Burney's father was an intellectual and middle-class member of an urban elite. For the upper classes in England the latter half of the eighteenth century was a period of increasing wealth and leisure. Life became more civilised and refined. It was a period during which the women of these classes in particular had more leisure, when their many domestic duties were taken over by servants or outside labour and they had far more time for leisure pursuits or self-improvement.

In addition, women of these classes were better educated than they had ever been before. 'All our ladies read now, which is a great extension', commented Dr Johnson in 1778.[1] Indeed, in some respects young women were arguably getting a better education than their privileged brothers, who were sent off to schools which gave them a rigid classical education, to be followed perhaps by the even narrower disciplines involved in preparing for a life in the Church or at the Bar. By the late eighteenth century the curriculum in girls' boarding schools not only covered the traditional female accomplishments, such as music, dancing, drawing and needlework, but also taught writing, grammar, arithmetic, geography and history, French and current affairs. 'Boys at grammar school,' remarked Mrs Eliza Fox, 'are taught Latin and Greek, despise the simpler paths of learning, and are generally ignorant of really useful matters of fact, about which a girl is much better informed.'[2]

By the end of the eighteenth century there was a consensus of opinion on the ideal education for women from the landed classes and the upper bourgeoisie. She was not frivolous, but neither was she a blue-stocking who threatened men on their own ground by being educated in the classics. She was sufficiently well-informed to make an agreeable companion for her husband and to educate her young children in the early years. Among the Bennet sisters in *Pride and Prejudice* Mary the blue-stocking represents one undesirable extreme, giddy Kitty and Lydia the other, whilst Jane and Elizabeth, as the plot proves, are admirably equipped to make desirable wives for the landed gentry.

Women of these social classes were not, of course, expected or educated to earn their own living or follow a profession of any sort. They were educated purely and simply to meet the rising expectations of domestic life. But as it happened, a high proportion of women from these classes remained unmarried at this period, and the sort of education they received was far from being unsuitable for an embryo novelist.

One of the reasons that Richardson, writing in the mid-eighteenth century, chose to identify with heroines rather than heroes in his novels, was the fact that, as a relatively humble printer, he had not had the benefit of a classical education. While Fielding and Smollett took over the picaresque novel as it had been developed by Cervantes and made use of classical allusions in their work, Richardson was very much aware of his limitations in being able to read only works which had appeared in English, something that put him 'down among the women', who were writing romances and despised domestic novels. It was a situation that put him very much on the defensive, and in *Sir Charles Grandison* he, not unnaturally, minimises the value of a classical education. Harriet Byron thinks the value of Latin is over-rated, while Miss Clements remarks drily that 'Something . . . should be left for *men* to excel in.' But it is of course a man who delivers the definitive words of wisdom and judgement. Mr Reeves, brought in as arbitrator in the discussion, first reads a quotation which begins: 'I have often thought it a great error to waste young gentlemen's years so long in learning Latin' and goes on to say that 'there is much noble knowledge to be had in the English and French languages: geography, history, chiefly that of our own country, the knowledge of nature, and the more *practical* parts of the mathematics . . . may make a gentleman very knowing, though he has not a word of Latin.' And then adds: 'And why, I would fain know, not a gentlewoman?' quoting Locke as an authority to prove that female education is a good thing.[3]

When Richardson's novel came out in 1753 the subject of women's education was still controversial, but by the end of the century it was widely accepted that a non-specific, general education of this kind was a good thing for gentlewomen. It must be emphasised that, for all his sympathies, Richardson was no feminist. The rider added by his spokesman Mr Reeves was to hold good for many decades to come:

> Be not therefore, ladies, ashamed either of your talents or acquirements. Only take care you give not up any knowledge that is more laudable in your sex, and more useful, for learning; and then I am sure you will, you *must*, be the more agreeable, the more suitable companions for it, to men of sense.

Although the education of women as wives and mothers may seem inadequate to us, it was nevertheless an important beginning. It raised the status of women, so that men no longer regarded them as mere breeders and domestic drudges. And, once the process of education has begun, it is unstoppable. A taste of knowledge inevitably breeds a hunger for more.

Until the eighteenth century marriage, like life, had tended to be brutish and short. In upper class families, indeed, in any families which owned property to be passed down, marriages were arranged, and affection between the partners was not a serious consideration. The death rate was such that most marriages were anyhow of short duration, and since children were liable to die young there was no strong affective bond between parents and children either. But by the mid-eighteenth century there had been a great improvement in health and domestic hygiene, and upper-class homes were more airy and spacious than they had ever been before. Women and children had a greater life expectancy, and wives were relieved from the traditional domestic chores – industrial processes had removed some of them, and servants took care of the rest. As a result families had more time, both for leisure pursuits and for each other. The ideal of domestic affection was now seen as a prime goal in life for both men and women, and for the landed gentry, where the husband did not have to follow a profession and stay away from home for long periods, it was an achievable goal. Fielding portrayed this ideal as early as 1742 in *Joseph Andrews*. Mr Wilson, who turns out to be the hero's long lost father, portrays a life-style which Joseph himself is destined to follow when he marries his Fanny:

> . . . we are seldom asunder during the residue of the day . . . for I am neither ashamed of conversing with my wife nor of playing with my children: to say the truth, I do not perceive that inferiority

of understanding which the levity of rakes, the dulness of men of business, or the austerity of the learned, would persuade us of in women. As for my woman, I declare I have found none of my own sex capable of making juster observations on life, or of delivering them more agreeably; nor do I believe any one possessed of a faithfuller or braver friend. And sure as this friendship is sweetened with more delicacy and tenderness, so it is confirmed by dearer pledges than can attend the closest male alliance; for what union can be so fast as our common interest in the fruits of our embraces?[4]

The ideal of companionate marriage portrayed from the time of Fielding to the time of Edgeworth and Austen was essentially based on the country life enjoyed by the landed gentry, where co-operation and companionship between husband and wife was still a real possibility. A century later the bourgeois novel typically portrayed a situation where domestic harmony was threatened by the husband's professional commitments and the wife's isolation in the home.

If husbands and wives were to be companions they clearly had to have some liking for each other, some affinity or sympathy. Mr Wilson speaks of friendship, and affection rather than passionate love was thought to be the proper basis of marriage. Although considerations of property were still important, it was generally felt that, as long as a couple had enough to live on comfortably, affection rather than fortune should govern choice in marriage.

For a time, a favourite theme in fiction was a conflict of interests between parents, who wanted their children to marry for gain, and children who wanted to marry for love. In 1749 Fielding set out the two views of marriage in *Tom Jones*, where Squire Western is determined to marry his daughter to a rich man of his choice, whilst Squire Allworthy thinks that love should be the foundation of marriage. The honourable compromise of the time, which is the position taken by Sophia, is that she will marry a man of her choice, but not without her father's consent. Innumerable novels would revolve on the withholding of parental consent, whilst the possibility of marriage for love led women to dreams of upward mobility through marriage, dreams rather unwholesomely fostered by fiction.

But writers of the eighteenth century drew a clear distinction between affection based on knowledge and judgement, and sexual desire, which was definitely thought to be a very bad reason for marriage, one of the reasons Fielding poured such scorn on *Pamela*. In his parody *Shamela* (1741) he wrote:

> The character of Shamela will make young gentlemen wary how they take the most fatal step both to themselves and families, by youthful, hasty, and improper matches; indeed, they may assure themselves that all such prospects of happiness are vain and delusive, and that they sacrifice all the solid comforts of their lives, to a very transient satisfaction of a passion, which how hot so ever it be, will be soon cooled; and when cooled, will afford them nothing but repentance. . . . Young gentlemen are here taught, that to marry their mother's chambermaids, and to indulge the passion of lust, at the expense of reason and common sense, in an act of religion, virtue, and honour; and, indeed, the surest road to happiness.

Certainly *Pamela* is a rather extreme tale of a woman's upward mobility through marriage. Most humble maidens who look too high are riding for a fall.

Given this new freedom, and its attendant pitfalls, the selection of a marriage partner who was both suitable and lovable was bound to become a dominant theme in fiction, and one to which women writers and readers particularly addressed themselves. After all, for a woman it was the single most important choice of a lifetime, very often the only moment of choice, and much more depended on her decision, for good or ill, than could ever be the case for a man. Her whole future happiness depended on attracting and choosing the right man. And, given the new freedom from parental authority, guilt and self-reproach were an added ingredient in the misery that followed a misguided choice. No wonder so many women writers addressed themselves to the problem with such didactic fervour.

But by the middle of the eighteenth century many upper-class women never married. During the eighteenth century there was a high proportion of lifelong bachelors amongst the younger sons of the nobility and gentry, who could not afford to get married and still maintain their life-style. Property arrangements had become very rigid, estates were entailed, and younger sons were now pushed out into the world with a small annuity and some hope of advancement through patronage. If they went into one of the professions it might take many years before they accumulated enough capital to maintain a household in the style to which they were accustomed by birth.

The proportion of sons, including some eldest sons, who were still unmarried at the age of fifty rose to twenty per cent in the last quarter of the eighteenth century, whilst the median age of marriage amongst the sons of the upper and professional classes had risen to twenty-eight by the year 1800.[5] By the middle of the eighteenth century Richardson, in *Sir Charles Grandison*, is already commenting through the pen of his heroine:

> I believe there are more bachelors now in England, by many thousands, than were a few years ago: and, probably, the numbers of them, (and of single women, of course) will every year increase. The luxury of the age will account a good deal for this; and the turn our sex take in *un*-domesticating themselves, for a good deal more.[6]

This passage reflects social trends already mentioned: higher living standards amongst the upper classes and the fact that wives had become something more (and more expensive) than domestic servants. If the analysis was at least partly correct, Richardson's prognosis certainly was. By 1773 *The Lady's Magazine* was complaining that nowadays 'the men marry with reluctance, sometimes very late, and a great many are never married at all'.[7] By the end of the eighteenth century twenty-five per cent of upper-class women remained lifelong spinsters – no less than one in four. Half a century earlier Richardson's Harriet Byron, herself the recipient of innumerable proposals of marriage, regarded spinsterhood as an inevitable fate for many women: 'I think, as matters stand in this age, or indeed ever did stand, that those women who have joined with the men in their insolent ridicule of old maids, ought never to be forgiven'.

Upper-class women who remained unmarried were not destitute. Indeed, the lack of suitable husbands and the fact that marriage portions continued to rise amongst the landed classes, meant that it was often more prudent for a daughter to remain a lifelong spinster than to marry a man with no property or immediate prospects, and fathers were reluctant to give their dowried daughters away too cheaply. Any woman of sense would want to avoid the desperate manoeuvres to catch a bachelor so aptly portrayed in the wiles of Mrs Bennet, which seem rather less silly when we remember that she had five unportioned daughters and the family estate was entailed, a practical detail which the detached and misanthropic Mr Bennet tends, like other problems, to ignore.

But even though upper-class women who remained unmarried were not left destitute, the lack of marriage prospects was a catastrophe in other ways. Educated women were doomed to a life of enforced idleness. At a time when household management and domestic affairs had been turned over to stewards, women spent their time reading novels, going to the theatre, playing cards, paying formal visits, or going to balls and assemblies in the season. Great fun for a while, but intolerable for any intelligent woman after a time if there was no husband in prospect, with a promise of a changed lifestyle, and the responsibility of family and household. It was from the ranks of these upper-class women, the privileged but bored twenty-five per cent, who had gone through nine seasons and had nothing to look forward to but a tenth, women with educated minds, with time on their hands and no immediate prospect of change, that the first wave of distinguished women novelists emerged. Edgeworth, Austen and Burney were all unmarried at thirty, women with lively minds and time on their hands.

But women writers could not have come to the fore if there had not been a ready-made market, mainly provided by the very class from which they themselves came. The improved education of women and their increased leisure stimulated all forms of entertainment, but book publishing perhaps most of all. And, with no particular aim at self-improvement or specialised knowledge, it was novels that women mostly read. Cheaper paper and increased sales brought down the cost of publishing, and the spread of the circulating libraries catered for the needs of the growing number of educated and leisured women. The first such library was opened in Bath in 1725, London got one in 1739, and by the 1780s they were to be found in all the major market towns of England. By then the libraries were buying some 400 copies of an average printing of 1000 copies.

Clearly it was only a question of time before some of these women readers, having read countless novels, said to themselves: 'I could do this' and had a go. If she was still single, still scribbling and with time on her hands by the age of twenty-seven or so, the likelihood was, she would succeed in producing something publishable. With novel sales booming, a publisher would be only too happy to accept a manuscript which met the needs of the market (and early women's novels, particularly Austen's, show strong signs of inbreeding), especially if the anonymous author could be bought off for a modest outlay of £20 or £30. Which, being young ladies of leisure, they usually could be.

2. Finding a Structure

ALTHOUGH women had been writing novels throughout the eighteenth century, they formed a sort of literary sub-culture. Stupid romances for stupid women, was how the male-dominated cultural elite of the period dismissed this steady output. Numerically, women novelists were already in the majority, but in terms of prestige and respect they were nowhere. Denigrating the output of women writers and its effects on female readers was something of a national pastime. It was considered a cause for concern, much as nowadays parents and educationalists worry about the effects of comics and television on the young.

As a result the kind of educated upper-class woman who might be attracted to writing at the latter end of the eighteenth century was put on the defensive. She might try and fend off criticism by treating the whole activity as a joke, or she could try to justify herself by claiming to provide an antidote to the poisonous influence of bad women writers. As we shall see, women novelists tried both these methods of self-defence.

At the same time, aspiring women novelists could hardly begin to write novels in a literary and cultural vacuum, and as far as themes and preoccupations are concerned they had far more in common with writers like Eliza Haywood and Mary Davys, however despised by the male elite, than they could have with the most brilliant and successful male writers. The cultural divide between men and women was nowhere deeper than in the writing of novels during the eighteenth century, and the reasons are fairly obvious when one looks at male literary output of the period.

The dominant male novel form during the eighteenth century was the picaresque, and its most successful exponents were Fielding and Smollett. Now, clearly, for both practical and moral reasons, the picaresque form was quite unsuitable for women writers. It was quite unthinkable for young ladies, and therefore young heroines, to wander about the countryside having bawdy adventures, or, indeed, adventures of any kind. It might be desirable for young heroes to show their mettle by getting into scrapes and sowing a few wild oats amongst serving wenches and bawds, but it certainly would not do for young heroines, for whom ignorance was usually equated with innocence, and who never stepped beyond the threshold without being carefully chaperoned. As we shall see, some women did develop a female variation of the picaresque novel: in the Gothic novel the heroine does have distinctly unladylike adventures, but she is an innocent victim, and therefore not responsible for her own odyssey. Thus the demands of fantasy are reconciled with the demands of morality.

But the Gothic novel was not a direct offspring of the male picaresque novel. Rather it was an elaboration of the female novel of seduction and betrayal. There were two main themes open to the women novelists of the eighteenth century, and they were like different sides of the same coin: the conduct-in-courtship novel, and the novel of misconduct, of seduction, betrayal and ruin. One was an exemplar for young ladies to follow, the other a dreadful warning.

Richardson, writing novels from the point of view of women, inevitably had to oppose the one-sided male morality expressed in the picaresque novel. From seducers and would-be seducers who either married or destroyed his heroines he went on to portray Sir Charles Grandison, the ultimate lady's man, always a gentleman, always fit for the drawing room, adored by all well-bred women for his perfect manners and morality. Sir Charles has never had anything in common with Tom Jones; one cannot imagine him having ever tried to seduce a servant girl below stairs. Richardson rejects the double standard, and in *Sir Charles Grandison* he constantly refutes the popular notion that reformed rakes make good husbands. He refutes the idea of a double standard for men, practising one set of manners and morals with women, in the parlour, and another amongst themselves. Harriet Byron says firmly that 'I should have a mean opinion of a man, who allowed himself to talk, even to *men*, what a woman might not hear.'[1]

Richardson's attitude was to gain increasing support during the second half of the eighteenth century, probably on account of the social changes described in the last chapter. If upper-class domestic life was becoming more civilised, then men also had to become more civilised. If women were being educated to become companions to their husbands, it followed that men also had to change somewhat, to become fit companions for their wives. Tenderness, kindness and sensibility were increasingly regarded as male virtues, and the Man of Sentiment made his appearance in fiction. It was a fiction that, at least in theory, did not condone the sexual double standard. And, of course, as far as the novel is concerned, it must not be overlooked that a growing female readership offered literary opportunities to male novelists as well as female ones. Fielding and his admirers might scoff at Richardson, but not only was there an increase in women readers who would choose his work in preference, but a growing number of fond and anxious fathers who, in opening their libraries for their daughters to use, must have felt that Richardson was far more suitable for general family entertainment than Fielding or Smollett.

The argument between Richardson and Fielding became one of morality rather than literary structure. Richardson, himself a pious Christian, objected to *Tom Jones* on moral grounds, and expected his own books to serve a didactic purpose. Certainly *Sir Charles Grandison* could be called the most comprehensive conduct novel of all time. When Dr Johnson appeared to lend his considerable weight to the Richardsonian side, there could be no doubt that the scales would ultimately come down in his favour. Writing to *The Rambler* in 1750, he sees fiction as dangerous fodder for the young, very much the attitude taken at the time on the novels written for young women:

> These books are written chiefly to the young, the ignorant, and the idle, to whom they serve as lectures of conduct, and introductions into life. They are the entertainments of minds unfurnished with ideas, and therefore easily susceptible of impressions; not fixed by principles, and therefore easily following the current of fancy; not informed by experience, and consequently open to every false suggestion and partial account.[2]

It therefore followed 'that nothing indecent should be suffered to approach their eyes or ears'. Selectivity rather than realism is to be the aim of fiction: 'If the world be promiscuously described, I cannot see of what use it can be to read the account'. The 'use' of fiction being 'to initiate youth by mock encounters in the art of necessary defence, and to increase prudence without impairing virtue'. While conceding that it is necessary for vice to be depicted, he emphasises that it should 'always disgust', and it is 'to be steadily inculcated, that virtue is the highest proof of understanding, and the only solid basis of greatness'.

Johnson's essay reveals a certain contempt for fiction and the readers of fiction. Although he does not mention women, he must have been perfectly well aware that women were the main consumers of new novels, and the paternal, protective didacticism he favours was to become the prevailing attitude to the 'problem' of women's addiction to novels. Writing so soon after the publication of *Roderick Random* (1748) and *Tom Jones* (1749), both of which enjoyed great popularity, it is not improbable that Johnson was coming down in favour of Richardson in the literary and moral debate which was going on between these authors.

In a sense we are talking about the feminisation of literary taste, and Richardson was winning the argument anyhow. Fielding may have found *Pamela* sufficiently ridiculous to parody it, but he admired *Clarissa* (1747–8) enough to be influenced by it. After its publication Fielding published *Amelia* (1752), much admired by Fanny Burney's father, and Smollett wrote *Ferdinand Count Fathom* (1753), both novels in which attempted seduction and the machinations of an intriguing rake are treated with a new seriousness.

The moral division between Fielding's picaresque novel and the epistolary novel of Richardson is illustrated very clearly in Maria Edgeworth's *Ormond* (1817). Edgeworth was unusual for her period in being as interested in the moral development of her male characters as in her female ones and her hero, Harry Ormond, is a good-hearted but raw young man who gradually becomes wiser and better. It is a *Bildungsroman*, and Harry's behaviour is strongly influenced by the novels he reads. (Edgeworth, like Dr Johnson and all the women novelists of her period, was quite sure that novels influenced behaviour for good or ill.) First of all *Tom Jones* falls into his hands, and he immediately identifies with its hero:

. . . he was charmed by the character – that of a warm-hearted, generous, imprudent young man, with little education, no literature, governed more by feeling than by principle, never upon any occasion reasoning, but keeping right by happy moral instincts; or when going wrong, very wrong, forgiven easily by the reader and by his mistress, and rewarded at the last with all that love and fortune can bestow, in consideration of his being – a very fine fellow.

Closing the book, Harry Ormond resolved to be what he admired – and if possible to shine forth an Irish Tom Jones. For this purpose he was not at all bound to be a moral gentleman, nor, as he conceived, to be a *gentleman* at all . . . he might begin by being an accomplished – blackguard.[3]

Ormond starts off his career as an Irish Tom Jones by trying to seduce a village maiden, but is saved from going too far when he discovers that a local lad loves the girl and wants to marry her. Shortly after this Harry reads *Sir Charles Grandison* and finds a new hero to emulate, one who:

> touched the nobler feelings of our young hero's mind, inspired him with virtuous emulation, made him ambitious to be a *gentleman* in the best and highest sense of the word. In short, it completely counteracted in his mind the effect of Tom Jones – all the generous feelings which were so congenial to his own nature, and which he had seen combined in Tom Jones, as if necessarily, with the habits of an adventurer, a spendthrift, and a rake, he now saw united with high moral and religious principles, in the character of a man of virtue, as well as a man of honour; a man of cultivated understanding and accomplished manners . . . Ormond has often declared that *Sir Charles Grandison* did him more good than any fiction he ever read in his life.[4]

Jane Austen, in *Northanger Abbey*, which is essentially a novel about the novel, and its influence on everyday life, also gives a special mention to *Sir Charles Grandison*. It is a book which Catherine Morland's mother is in the habit of reading, and which is 'not like *Udolpho* at all'.[5]

With the feminisation of literature in the second half of the eighteenth century, and the emphasis on sentiment and sensibility, for which the Richardsonian epistolary novel was such a suitable vehicle, went an explicit reaffirmation of Christian values and a new didacticism. With so many women reading and writing novels moral content was a form of self-justification, the only defence against the charge that women scribblers were filling young girls' heads full of romantic nonsense. Novelists like Eliza Haywood claimed that their stories of sexual seduction and abduction, of imprisonment and remorse, were written as a warning to young ladies. A rather more convincing case can be made for the novels on courtship and marriage, which told young ladies how to conduct themselves along the short but tricky path from schoolroom to altar.

Really women writers only had two basic plots, and both were related to sex. There was the tragic plot of seduction and betrayal, and the comic plot of courtship and marriage. Richardson, in choosing to write from the woman's point of view, only had these two plots to choose from and exploited them to the full in *Clarissa* and *Sir Charles Grandison*. *Pamela* is something of a hybrid, a potential tragedy of seduction and imprisonment which turns into a comedy when B. marries his victim instead of destroying her.

But neither *Pamela* nor *Clarissa* could provide suitable models for aspiring women novelists. Writers like Burney and Austen were definitely not addressing themselves to chambermaids, but to the women of the upper and middle classes, and such extremes of upward mobility through marriage as described in *Pamela* would have seemed both disgusting and alarming to their readership. At a time when young ladies were finding it so hard to catch an eligible bachelor, the story of a servant girl's virtue being rewarded through marriage would not have been amusing. Nor was *Clarissa* a model which endeared itself to women novelists, who did not choose to portray heroines as the helpless victims of men. When they did portray women as the victims of rakes and seducers, their heroines put up a hard struggle and almost always got the better of their persecutors. The Gothic novel is one development of the novel of abduction: in *The Mysteries of Udolpho*, written by a woman, the heroine shows great initiative in resisting the villain and finally escapes unscathed; in Lewis's *The Monk* the women are helpless victims of the machinations of men and die, or are rescued at the last moment by men.

This leaves *Sir Charles Grandison*, a comic novel of manners and marriage, as the one male novel with which women novelists, anxious to disassociate themselves from the great mass of despised female writers, could identify, the one to which they could pay homage and use as an exemplar. Writers of the generation of Burney, Edgeworth and Austen were not feminist revolutionaries. Trying to accept the world as it was, and teach their readers to adapt to the standards of a male world in order to survive, they had little use for the tragic outlook. Only by adopting a detached comic voice could they hope to give conviction and consistency to their portrayal of a world where they and their heroines were required to obey and submit without question.

But even *Sir Charles Grandison*, in spite of its gentility, its sympathy for women, its emphasis on tact and delicacy and good manners, proved an unsatisfactory model for later women novelists as far as structure was concerned. The epistolary style, which Richardson associated with the female voice – subjective, emotional, and suggestive of a highly sedentary way of life – proved to be one which women novelists rarely used, and then almost always badly, for the same reason as they avoided the tragic mode. A woman who is trying to come to terms with a world and with values where she is object and not subject, an outsider, regarded as an inferior dependant with no rights or voice of her own, must at all costs avoid the subjective voice if she is to conform to standard morality and at the same time remain in control of her material. Conformity was required of her both on a personal level and as an author, and in this situation she is at her best when she employs the detached irony of the authorial third person. Richardson, as a man who had no doubt of the ultimate superiority of his own sex, could afford subjective outpourings on the part of his female heroines. A woman writer could not.

Burney did use the epistolary form with great success in *Evelina*, but she severely restricts her heroine's self-expression and uses the form more to contrast the voices of innocence and experience. The very fact that her heroine is so young and naive assures the author an ironic detachment. Edgeworth wrote one epistolary novel, *Leonora*, easily her dullest novel and said to have been written in that form to please a man who wanted to marry her. Austen, after her juvenile burlesques of the epistolary novel, tried the form again in *Lady Susan*, was clearly not at home with the form, and abandoned the book. Perhaps she was also partly influenced by the fact that *Leonora* was published in 1806, just about the time she was writing *Lady Susan*, and has a very similar plot.

One is forced to the conclusion that women writers, while admiring *Sir Charles Grandison* as the most ladylike novel ever written by a man, really did not learn very much from Richardson, and owed far more to the despised women novelists who were always being sneered at by men. Anxious to disassociate themselves from such female romancers, who certainly lacked artistry, they found that Richardson's novel provided a convenient status symbol, a link with the great male tradition. Austen could hardly have made Catherine Morland's mother read Eliza Haywood in preference to Mrs

Radcliffe, and yet for her own purposes she was an avid reader of women's novels from an early age, as her juvenile burlesques show.

In terms of presenting a conformist morality suitable for young ladies, women novelists from Burney on took much more from their female predecessors than from any male writer. Enforced conformity brings a certain narrowness with it, if the conformity is to be reasonably consistent. Richardson, as a man, could raise issues and female dilemmas without ever really resolving them, whereas women writers were chary of opening such a Pandora's box. So, in the courtship novel, they stuck to fairly narrow issues: a young lady must not be seen in improper company; a young lady must not play the coquette; a young lady must choose her husband on rational grounds, and trust her judgement rather than her emotions; a young lady must not read too many novels of the wrong sort, particularly foreign ones, and base her perception of reality on fiction; a young lady must not be frivolous, vain, extravagant, or have unrealistic expectations of life; above all, a young lady must guard her reputation more dearly than life itself.

Such values are implicit rather than explicit in Richardson. As a man, he treats such matters almost jokingly, as when Harriet Byron is so desperately ashamed of having been to a masquerade, an entertainment which leads to her abduction and her final rescue by Sir Charles. For the most part Richardson addresses himself to rather more serious problems affecting women, but always with the ultimate complacency of a man who regards women as soft, gentle creatures to be guided and guarded by men. So, in the first volume, Richardson has his heroine sigh to her confidante: 'In what a situation, Lucy, are we women? – If we have some little genius, and have taken pains to cultivate it, we must be thought guilty of affectation, whether we appear desirous to conceal it, or submit to have it called forth.'[6] But when she is abducted Harriet behaves like a weak helpless female, fainting when Sir Charles comes to the rescue and repeatedly crying 'Save me! save me!' Almost symbolically, Sir Charles says: 'Will you, madam, put yourself into my protection?' and gets the answer: 'O yes, yes, yes, with my whole heart – Dear, good sir, protect me.'[7] Later, relating the incident to a relative of Harriet's, Sir Charles says modestly: 'You see, Mr Reeves, what an easy conquest this was.' Though he is nominally referring to the conquest of the villain, the reader inevitably thinks of his conquest of Harriet herself. Now, although women novelists continued to make use of abductions in their plots, they did so to show their heroines showing courage and initiative in getting themselves out of trouble. 'Run mad as often as you chuse; but do not faint' the fifteen-year-old Jane Austen wrote in her burlesque of the epistolary novel.[8] Charlotte Smith's Emmeline persuades her abductor to take her back; Mary Brunton's heroine in *Self-Control* soon began 'to regain the confidence which strong minds naturally put in their own exertions' and planned her escape.

At the beginning of the second volume of *Sir Charles Grandison* Harriet Byron raises another problem peculiar to women of the period:

What can a woman do who is addressed by a man of talents inferior to her own? Must she throw away her talents? Must she hide her light under a bushel, purely to do credit to a man? She cannot pick and choose, as men can. She has only her negative; and if she is desirous to oblige her friends, not always *that*. Yet it is said, women must not encourage fops and fools. They must encourage men of sense only. And it is *well* said. But what will they do, if their lot be cast only among the foplings? If men of sense do not offer themselves?[9]

The problem is exemplified in the character of Charlotte Grandison, a wit who does not suffer fools gladly, and easily the most entertaining character in the book. Sir Charles, who is a great maker of marriages and is anxious to get his sisters married off as quickly as possible, is constantly reproving her for her lively spirits and rather cynical wit. Speaking of marriage, he tells her: 'If control is *likely* to be necessary, it will be with women with such charming spirits as you know whose, Charlotte'.[10] After a somewhat stormy beginning to a marriage with a man who is clearly her intellectual inferior, Charlotte succumbs reluctantly to domestic bliss. She never loses her ironic tone, which makes such good reading, but we are to understand that she is now a happy and contented woman with her doting fool of a husband, even if she is not quite prepared to admit it. This is a male solution to the problem, if one can call it a solution, and really fudges the issue. Charlotte Lucas's acceptance of Mr Collins as a husband states the problem much more frankly.

But of course *Sir Charles Grandison* does fall into the female tradition of the comic conduct-in-courtship novel which provided the main line of development through the eighteenth century to the work of Jane Austen. Sir Charles himself stands in a long line of suitors who were also mentors of female conduct, a line which stretches from the male lover of *The Reform'd Coquet* by Mary Davys in 1724 to Mr Knightley in *Emma*.

3. Anxious Apologies

'I SUPPOSE Mrs Morland objects to novels' Isabella surmises about Catherine's mama, as the two girls discussed the merits of *Udolpho* in *Northanger Abbey*. 'Objecting to novels' was an all too familiar stance of an older generation of women towards the diversions of the young. Parents and guardians worried about young women's addiction to fiction as though it were a drug, and this is reflected in the fiction itself. Hardly a novel appeared which did not express, either directly or indirectly, the view that young women should not read too many novels. Sometimes the view was expressed directly by the author, sometimes in the speeches of a character of authority. Since such views were themselves being expressed within the pages of a novel, this placed the author in something of a dilemma. Usually she extricated herself from her ambiguous situation by making a clear distinction between the kind of novel she was writing, and other types of fiction which she did consider harmful, misleading or silly. For women of Austen's generation the novels most often selected for blame in turning the heads of young women and poisoning their minds were usually foreign, the French or German products of the new Romanticism. Rousseau's *La Nouvelle Héloïse* is the favourite object of scorn, with Goethe's *Werther* coming a close second. Women authors tried to deflect criticism from their own productions by focusing the prevailing critical attitudes to the many novels being read, and written, by women, which they could not ignore and to some extent had to reflect, on work which they considered unlike their own.

One result of this anxious ambiguity which women writers felt with regard to their own work at this period was a tendency to exaggerate the differences between different types of novel. Modern readers of *The Mysteries of Udolpho*, whose prior knowledge of the book is only through the pages of *Northanger Abbey*, will be surprised to find that Mrs Radcliffe, like Austen herself, at all times preaches the importance of rational common sense in dealing with both the real and imagined terrors of the world. Another result of the defensive attitude women writers were forced to adopt in relation to their work was a tendency to become didactic in order to justify their activity. If, as was the constant complaint, too many young women were getting ludicrously romantic and unrealistic ideas from reading novels, having their heads turned or stuffed full of nonsense, the aspiring woman novelist could justify her work and disassociate herself from the great mass of second-rate female scribblers who were supposed to have done this harm by presenting a story which purported to be the vehicle of correct moral attitudes and would guard the young woman reader both from the folly of her own inexperience and the dangers of other people's fiction.

In this atmosphere, with women's fiction regarded as not only second-rate, something fit only for the amusement of other women, but liable to be positively harmful to its readership, they were easily put on the defensive. They tended to play safe, by reflecting conservative values. Scarcely daring to lay claim to that male preserve, literary merit, they tried to obviate the charge of frivolity by preaching duty, good sense and propriety to their audience of young ladies. In addition, many of them were not independent professional women, but dutiful daughters living at home, and so they had to avoid giving offence to their fathers, family and friends. The coercive quality of family affection, particularly of the father/daughter relationship at this time, could be the most destructive of all. It was to fathers that such aspiring young women writers owed their education, and loving gratitude could be crippling when it came to self-expression. Maria Edgeworth's early genius was subdued and diverted into more conventional channels by a father who regarded himself as her mentor.

During the last three decades of the eighteenth century there are many references, usually derogatory, to the flood of women's novels being written by women for women. In 1773 a writer in *The Lady's Magazine* complained that 'there is scarce a young lady in the kingdom who has not read with avidity a great number of romances and novels, which tend to vitiate the taste'. By 1796 *The Times* remarked satirically that 'four thousand and seventy-three novels are now in the press from the pens of young ladies of fashion'.[1] The subscription library had become a local centre where young ladies could acquire other feminine fripperies apart from novels. In Burney's *Camilla*, for instance, the heroine wins a trinket in a raffle there, the first of many financial embarrassments to overcome the inexperienced young girl. And in Austen's unfinished novel, *Sanditon*, the heroine is tempted by a drawer full of rings and brooches at the subscription library, which 'afforded . . . all the useless things in the world that could be done without'. But then the heroine picks up a book: 'it happened to be a volume of *Camilla*. She had not Camilla's youth, and had no intention of having her distress, – so she turned from the drawer of rings and brooches repressed farther solicitation and paid for what she bought.'[2] Austen knows *Camilla*, and clearly expects her readers to be equally familiar with the novel. This is typical of women's novels at this period. In spite of their defensiveness about being women writers, they constantly refer to other novels by women and clearly expect their readers to know what they are talking about. In this case, Austen is referring to an author she admires. Her heroine, we are given to understand, is a better and wiser young woman after reading *Camilla*, since she decides not to spend her money on unnecessary trifles. A defence of the right kind of novel, one which preached good sense and the importance of maidenly propriety. But examples of the deleterious effects of the wrong kind of novel, mostly foreign ones, are much easier to find in the novels of this period.

Young women without the economic necessity of earning a living might write their first novel, usually anonymously, with a great sense of freedom and enjoyment. But later, if they acquired a reputation, the social and moral pressure on them was enormous, even if insidious. One can see this kind of pressure being exerted on both Burney and Edgeworth, and in the case of both these writers their first book remained their best one.

Fanny Burney published *Evelina* as a youngish woman without the knowledge of her family. She did it, she claimed, for a 'frolic', and her father was not told she was the author until it had become a success. Of course she was aware of the opprobrium attached to the reading of novels by young women, and although her preface contains the usual defence, her tone is joking, almost ironic, and she certainly does not claim to be writing for the moral betterment of her readership:

Perhaps were it possible to effect the total extirpation of novels our young ladies in general, and boarding-school damsels in particular, might profit from their annihilation: but since the distemper they have spread seems incurable, since their contagion bids defiance to the medecine of advice or reprehension, and since they are found to baffle all the mental art of physic, save what is prescribed by the slow regimen of Time, and bitter diet of Experience, surely all attempts to contribute to the number of those which may be read, if not with advantage, at least without injury, ought rather to be encouraged than condemned.

But a decade later, when she was writing *Camilla*, Burney's attitude is very different. By this time she was famous, her identity known, and like so many women writers at this time, her attitude to public recognition was ambiguous, since women had been taught from childhood not to seek the limelight, to be modest, domestic and withdrawn. Burney's anxiety about public reaction to her writing, exacerbated by the fact that she moved in high society, both intellectual and aristocratic, was made worse during the writing of *Camilla* by the fact that she had recently married a penniless French refugee and desperately wanted the book to earn money to support herself and her husband. This is a factor which can have a crucial effect on the ultimate tone and quality of a book, and during this period the commercial imperative tended to have a deleterious effect on women's writing. Luckily Jane Austen never had to support herself by writing. But Burney did, and the tone of playful irony she used in the apologia in the preface of her first novel has now changed to real anxiety. She wrote to her father in June 1795 about the composition of *Camilla*: 'I own I do not like calling it a *Novel*: it gives so simply the notion of a mere love story, that I recoil a little from it. I mean it to be *sketches of Characters & morals, put in action*, not a Romance.'[3] She was reassured when Dr Burney praised it as 'the best system of *Education*, I ever saw'. The book was, by gracious permission, dedicated to the Queen, and when Burney visited Windsor she made a point of explaining to the Princesses that in *Camilla* 'Politics' were, *all ways*, left out' on the grounds that 'they were not a *feminine* subject for discussion'.[4]

Jane Austen rejected the blandishments of the Prince Regent with a laugh, but Burney's relationship with the Royal Family put her in a rather peculiarly embarrassing position. The awarding of a post in the Royal Household as a recognition for authorship hardly seems a suitable recompense to us, and Burney was unhappy at Court, but by the time she published *Camilla* she had good reason to be anxious about retaining the royal favour. Apart from her literary earnings her only income was a small pension from the Royal Family.

Fearful of losing her small pension of £400 per year, Burney worried in case the Royal Family should disapprove of her marriage to a Frenchman. But it was Dr Burney who violently opposed the marriage, pretending to her and to himself that D'Arblay's lack of fortune was the reason. In fact, like Edgeworth's father, he was proud of his daughter, and all his life tried to retain some intellectual and moral, as well as emotional, hold on his daughter. Men like Dr Burney and Richard Lovell Edgeworth found in daughters who were gifted and did not leave home an intellectual companionship that their marriages had almost certainly lacked. They saw such daughters as extensions of themselves, to be guided and moulded by their wishes. In October 1791, when she was almost forty years old, Fanny Burney wrote to her sister of her father:

> . . . I now live with him wholly; he has himself appropriated me a place, a seat, a desk, a table, & every convenience & comfort, & he never seemed yet so earnest to keep me about him. We read together, write together, chat – compare notes, communicate projects, & diversify each other's employments. He is all goodness, gaiety, & sweetest affection – & his society & kindness are more precious to me than ever.
>
> Fortunately, in this season of leisure & comfort, the Spirit of Composition proves active. The Day is never long enough, & I could employ two pens almost incessantly in merely scribbling what will not be repressed. This is a delight to my dear Father inexpressibly great: & though I have gone no further than to let him know, from time to time, the *species* of Matter that occupies me, he is perfectly contented, & patiently waits till something is quite finished, before he insists upon reading a word.[5]

Burney was nevertheless a good deal more independent of her father's domination than Edgeworth, though his approval of her writing was always highly important to her, and his bitter opposition to her marriage caused her considerable distress.

In the case of Edgeworth we see a much more thorough and damaging domination by her father, which seems all the more tragic because Edgeworth's gifts as a writer were much greater than Burney's. Her first novel, *Castle Rackrent*, written without her father's knowledge or consent when she was only eighteen, shows real genius. Written quite outside the feminine tradition, it has a strength of language only to be matched by Emily Brontë nearly half a century later. Funny, earthy, irreverent and totally undidactic, utterly unladylike and more in the spirit of Sterne and Fielding than anything penned by a woman of that period, it is a brilliantly free piece of writing which inspired Scott when he came to write *Waverley* and might very well have inspired Emily Brontë too, if she had needed it. Half a century before the publication of *Wuthering Heights* the young Maria Edgeworth wrote a short novel with a first person narrator who is a servant speaking a broad regional dialect. But the book is inspired by a strong comic irony, a cynicism about social hierarchy and the machinery of government which is quite unique.

But Edgeworth, like so many women of the period, never left home, though her experience, for a woman, was broad. The move to the Irish estate when she was fifteen years old, an experience which inspired *Castle Rackrent*, led to a lifelong involvement with local people and the practicalities of estate management which is reflected in her novels. Edgeworth is unusual for her period in being able to describe the lives of men with as much conviction, indeed, almost more easily, than the lives of women. Later, as her fame grew, she travelled to France and Switzerland, met the famous in Parisian and London drawing rooms, enjoyed the friendship of her admirer Walter Scott, and became something of a surrogate mother or 'aunt' to her father's many children by his three wives after the early death of Maria's mother. Edgeworth, Burney, the Brontës and Mrs Gaskell all lost their mothers in early childhood, a situation which tends to strengthen the emotional and perhaps more intellectual bonds with the father, whilst removing the constraints to feminine conformity which a mother so often imposes.

But in the case of Edgeworth her father's interest in her doings became an intellectual tyranny, though Maria herself never saw it as such. He seems to have been a vain, egotistical man, for whom Maria's achievements only added to his own fame as a writer and intellectual. His overbearing egotism was obvious to those who met him, and Byron commented, on meeting them both: 'One would never have guessed she could write *her name*; whereas her father talked, *not* as if he could write nothing else, but as if nothing else was worth writing.'[6]

As we have seen, many women of Maria's social standing remained unmarried during the period of her youth, but Maria had particular problems as a woman, as she never grew to normal stature, and was almost dwarflike. This, together with the early death of her mother, may have made her abnormally dependent on her father, so malleable to his influence. But of course any woman living at home, without independent resources, is bound to be influenced by those in authority, and the authority of someone who is loved and respected is the most insidious. The anarchic *Castle Rackrent*, written without her father's knowledge, was published in 1800. From then on she was, like so many women of the period, coerced into didacticism, and in Edgeworth's case the main influence was undoubtedly her father, who vetted everything she wrote and regarded himself as her teacher and mentor.

A year after the publication of *Castle Rackrent* she published some *Moral Tales* for children, and a second novel, *Belinda*. In this book some brilliant characterisation of high society life is spoiled by a strong didactic theme and the book appears with the apologia which seems to be almost *de rigeur* for women novelists who do not wish to lose the respect of men:

> The following work is offered to the public as a Moral Tale – the author not wishing to acknowledge a Novel. Were all novels like those of madame de Crousaz, Mrs. Inchbald, miss Burney, or Dr. Moore, she would adopt the name of novel with delight. But so much folly, errour, and vice are disseminated in books classed under this denomination, that it is hoped the wish to assume another title will be attributed to feelings that are laudable, and not fastidious.

And the text of *Belinda* is peppered with derogatory comments on novels, the difference between novels and real life, and the bad effects novels can have on young girls. So, for instance, we are told that a girl eloped at the age of sixteen because she had been 'spoiled by early novel-reading'.

This change of direction, stronger at this period and more self-conscious than later, though the didactic strain had come to stay, was clearly due to her father's influence. In 1805 she wrote to Sophy Ruxton that it was Richard Lovell Edgeworth who had told her that 'to be a mere writer of pretty stories and novelettes would be unworthy of his partner, pupil and daughter'. Edgeworth accepted his judgement; in a letter to the same correspondent written in the same year: 'Where should I be without my father? I should sink into that nothing from which he has raised me.'[7]

Later in her career Edgeworth narrowed her criticism of the novel to the evil influence of foreign romantic fiction. This was in line with a general trend of women writers during this period, when women justified their activity by claiming to provide an antidote of sense and realism to the disease of romantic flights of fancy induced by the reading of fiction. In Hannah More's *Cœlebs in Search of a Wife*, which was published in 1809 and reads more like a tract on correct female upbringing than a novel, we are told that:

> Mrs. Stanley lamented that novels, with a very few admirable exceptions, had done infinite mischief, by so completely establishing the omnipotence of love, that the young reader was almost systematically taught an unresisting submission to a feeling, because the feeling was commonly represented as irresistible.[8]

By preaching the necessity of sense in opposition to the romantic sensibility supposedly fostered in the bosoms of young women by a reading of too many, mainly foreign novels, women writers were able to justify their own activity and disassociate themselves from the despised generality of female romancers. By focusing critical attention on foreign literature as the source of wrong-headed ideas they not only deflected criticism from themselves, put it at a safe distance, but gave themselves some sort of stature by being the wholesome, homegrown product.

There are hints at the end of *Belinda* that Edgeworth will come to terms with her guilty ambiguity about writing novels, induced by society in general and her father in particular, by taking this way out. An unworthy suitor called Mr Vincent has been duly rejected by the heroine and has gone off to Germany. The fashionable Lady Delacour, a scintillating character who is really the core of the book, comments:

> Let him be as generous and as penitent as he pleases, I am heartily glad that he is on his way to Germany. I dare say he will find in the upper or *lower* circles of the empire some heroine in the Kotzebue taste, who will alternately make him miserable, till he is happy; and

happy till he is miserable. He is one of those men who require great emotions – Fine lovers these make for stage effect! – but the worst husbands in the world![9]

In Edgeworth's next novel, *Leonora*, published in 1806, the evil influence of foreign romantic fiction becomes a central theme. The plot concerns Leonora, a virtuous wife and mother who, from misguided generosity, invites a woman of scandalous reputation into her home. Lady Olivia had walked out of an unhappy marriage to find solace in the sublime beauties of Switzerland and in 'the bold genius and exquisite pathos of some German novelists I hold myself indebted for my largest portion of ideal bliss', adding, in this letter to her kind hostess, that 'I am well aware, my Leonora, that you approve not of these my favourite writers.'[10]

Leonora, ignoring both the warning implicit in this revelation of Lady Olivia's taste in fiction and the more explicit warnings of her own mother, decides to champion her return to society and invites her to stay, whereupon Lady Olivia shows her gratitude by seducing Leonora's husband and running away with him. In her early letters Olivia appears to be something of a feminist, who has shown her independence by behaving in an unconventional manner: 'Condemned to incessant hypocrisy, or everlasting misery, woman is the slave or the outcast of society . . . to what purpose have we understandings, which we may not use? hearts, which we may not trust? To our unhappy sex genius and sensibility are the most treacherous gifts of Heaven.'[11]

But Leonora's mother, the Duchess, who seems to the modern reader to be the epitome of conservatism, scotches all such arguments. She tells her daughter that 'of late years we have heard more of sentiment than of principles; more of the rights of woman than of her duties.' Strength of mind, she declares, is shown in resisting one's passions, not in yielding to them. She condemns Olivia's conduct and adds: 'The course of reading which her ladyship followed, was the certain preparation for her consequent conduct.'[12]

This course of reading conspicuously includes the *Sorrows of Werther* and *La Nouvelle Héloïse*. Olivia voices outrageous opinions, embarrassing Leonora by speaking out in favour of divorce. In one of her own letters the scandalous lady criticises her hostess as *'too English* – far too English for one who has known the charms of French ease, vivacity and sentiment' and goes on to praise the dazzling life of flirtation and gallantry led by French women after marriage. 'In England' she complains 'gallantry is not yet *systematized*, and our sex look more to their families than to what is called *society*'.[13] Like Hannah More's heroine in *Cœlebs*, Leonora is compared to Milton's Eve, a natural, unassuming woman who does not try to please any man other than her husband.

But, we are given to understand, high-flown foreign fiction has little to do with real life and does not help us to live it. The Duchess remains confident that her daughter will win her husband back, and she is right. Leonora's husband grows tired of Olivia's moods and tantrums, her 'morbid sensibility' and her need to be 'agitated by violent emotions'. He suspects, rightly, that she only loves him in so far as he bears some feeble resemblance to her fictional heroes, St Preux and Werther. 'But how can a plain Englishman hope to reach "The high sublime of deep absurd"?' When she is afraid that he is about to go back to his wife, Olivia imitates Héloïse's deathbed scene and threatens suicide, but her lover recognises the literary origins of her ruse, and finds the situation comic. When he falls ill the wronged Leonora defies the risk of infection to be with her husband, while Olivia excuses herself by claiming that 'my sensibility could not support the scene'. The prophecy of the Duchess to her daughter comes true: 'How many absurd heroines of romance, and of those who imitate them in real life, do we see, who can never act with common sense or presence of mind.'[14] Leonora's husband writes a farewell letter to Olivia in which he says 'You have completely convinced me that the character of a sober, or, if you please, a cold Englishman, is totally unsuited to exotic systems of gallantry.' Olivia goes abroad and the Duchess comments: 'England is not the place for women of her character.'

After *Belinda* and the even more explicit *Leonora* Edgeworth became much more relaxed in her attitude to her own craft; almost as though, having pinned the blame squarely on foreign fiction, she had exorcised her own anxiety and ambiguity.

Jane Austen also aligned herself with the doctrines implicitly and more often explicitly associated with these women's novels of sense. But she is much more restrained in assigning blame to the written word. In *Mansfield Park*, it is true, the young people transgress by performing an improper play, and the play is by Kotzebue, but there is no suggestion that Kotzebue is directly to blame for the subsequent misconduct of any characters in the book. Knowing the nature of the play, the young people should never have embarked on a performance. Indeed, amateur theatricals were in themselves an impropriety. In *Sense and Sensibility* it is youth and inexperience which are blamed for Marianne Dashwood's faults, not her reading habits. And in the one book where the heroine's literary tastes do appear to lead her astray Austen refuses to fall into the ambiguous trap which caught so many of her contemporaries:

> I will not adopt the ungenerous and impolitic custom, so common with novel writers, of degrading by their contemptuous censure the very performance to the number of which they are themselves adding – joining with their greatest enemies in bestowing the harshest epithets on such works, and scarcely ever permitting them to be read by their own heroine.[15]

And, instead of an attack or a feeble, self-decrying apologia, she launches into a spirited defence of the novel:

> there seems to be a general wish of decrying the capacity and undervaluing the labour of the novelist, and of slighting the performances which have only genius, wit, and taste to recommend them.

Novels, she goes on, are:

> work in which the greatest powers of the mind are displayed, in which the most thorough knowledge of human nature, the happiest delineation of its varieties, the liveliest effusions of wit and humour are conveyed to the world in the best chosen language.

Although *Northanger Abbey* is an early work, it was only published in 1818, after Austen's death, and when the need for such a defence had largely died away. Like the novel itself, the habit of decrying fiction, in which women joined with their enemies, belonged to Austen's youth. In 1778, the same year which saw the publication of *Evelina*, Jane Austen wrote to her sister:

> I have received a very civil note from Mrs Martin requesting my name as a Subscriber to her Library . . . .. As an inducement to subscribe Mrs Martin tells us that her Collection is not to consist

only of Novels, but of every kind of Literature &c. &c. – She might
have spared this pretension to *our* family, who are great Novel-
readers & not ashamed of being so . . . .[16]

Of course it was not only the Austen family who were avid fiction
readers. All the novels of the period are full of cross-references, and
their authors assume a comprehensive knowledge of contemporary
fiction in their readers, including the books which were supposed to
undermine character. *Northanger Abbey* assumes a knowledge of
Udolpho, in *Mansfield Park* the reader is expected to know the plot of
Kotzebue's *Lovers' Vows*, and even the plain Englishman in *Leonora* is
familiar enough with Rousseau to know when life is imitating art. If
the novel was an object of 'contemptuous censure' for so many years
it was principally because women had taken over the form and were
now its predominant exponents. If women could write novels, and
were doing so in such large numbers, it clearly followed that novel-
writing must be a trivial and silly occupation. Of course there were
plenty of bad women novelists, just as there have always been plenty
of bad male poets, but without bringing poetry into disrepute. As a
result women of intelligence and ability found themselves in
something of a double-bind when they began writing. They tried to
disassociate themselves from the run-of-the-mill writers; they took
refuge in a sense of social responsibility to justify their art; they
apologised in advance for the crime of writing novels, and did exactly
what Austen accused them of doing. But by the time Austen died in
1818 she and her female contemporaries had achieved enough, and
were sufficiently respected, to make her posthumous defence of the
novel unnecessary.

That does not mean, however, that women novelists were now
being regarded as the equals of men. When *Frankenstein* was published
in 1818 the author was generally assumed to be a man, possibly
Shelley himself. Reviewing *Valperga* in March 1823, *Blackwood's*
wrote that they had been in error in assuming it to be the work of Mr
rather than Mrs Shelley, 'and then we most undoubtedly said to
ourselves, "For a man it was excellent, but for a woman it was
wonderful."' Thirty years later Charlotte Brontë wrote that she and
her sisters had chosen ambiguous pseudonyms because 'we had a
vague impression that authoresses are liable to be looked on with
prejudice'.[17] The 'weapon of personality' she accuses critics of using
has not grown rusty since, nor has the habit of designating certain
modes of writing and thinking as 'feminine'.

4. Fanny Burney

ALTHOUGH *Evelina* is an epistolary novel it bears very little relationship to the work of Richardson and is highly innovative. It is short and pithy where Richardson is long and self-indulgent. The plot moves along at a fairly spanking pace and, instead of using the letter form to expose the sentiments of her heroine, blurring everything else, Burney uses the literary device to obtain contrasting voices, particularly between youth and age, innocence and experience, and to place her heroine clearly and succinctly in a very real social background. In *Sir Charles Grandison* the epistolary form is a very clumsy way of moving the story forward, and Richardson ends up by having a heroine who does little else but write letters, whilst other characters spend copious amounts of time copying letters and sending them to and fro. In *Evelina* the letters have an immediacy and credibility lacking in Richardson, are cleverly used to move the narrative forward, and one feels they might actually have been sent, which is never the case in Richardson, where the letter is always a literary device addressed to the reader rather than a recipient. And whilst Richardson was deeply conservative with a veneer of liberalism, Burney, as a woman, had a self-protective veneer of diehard conservatism under which lurked much more liberal, questioning attitudes which dared not find full expression.

At this period in time the comic mode was a self-protective mechanism for women writers. In *Evelina* there is a satiric conservatism which is highly ambiguous and allows the author to keep her private opinions to herself. Richardson, as a male writer, could wallow in what he imagined to be female sentiments, even allow his heroines to sigh a little on the injustice of a woman's lot, from the safety of his male identity. It did not impinge on his own experience, and there was no danger of such sentiments getting out of control, particularly as he never really questioned the fundamental position of the sexes in society and regarded the traditional attitudes to women as correct. Burney recognised that women's situation was not God-given and immutable but part of the social order, an order which the individual could not afford to challenge. She therefore gained a modicum of control by distancing herself from her heroine and placing her firmly within a framework of social convention. We see her moving as a novice through the world of balls, supper parties and assemblies, learning the correct behaviour; it is her reactions to these events which matter, not the secret beatings of her heart. And when she finds a husband he is first and foremost a trustworthy guide through this social labyrinth.

Sir Charles Grandison confirms all the traditional values concerning women's role, and the hero is such a paragon precisely because Richardson believed that men were the guardians and protectors of women. Sir Charles is constantly voicing his very conservative opinions on the proper conduct of women, and sees it as his duty to subdue his high-spirited sister Charlotte, who is cursed with a witty tongue and opinions of her own, and is singularly lacking in meekness and discretion. But at the same time Richardson is a Christian, and his hero projects Christian values. Some sins, we are told, should be left to the judgement of God, and human beings ought to be charitable. Sir Charles Grandison, for instance, admonishes his sisters for being hard and cruel to a 'fallen woman', the woman who was the mistress of their dead father in his later years, and who is certainly shown as a worthy object of his charity, being a tearful widow with children to support.

But Fanny Burney, as a woman, was very conscious that women's conduct was not judged by God, but by men, and not by men like Sir Charles Grandison either. In polite society, she knew, a woman could not afford to take chances with the only thing she possessed which was of value – her unsullied reputation. And it was a message which had to be forcibly conveyed to her female readers, if only to deflect the kind of charges being made against women's fiction as an unwholesome diet. As a result Burney and many of her female contemporaries often seem extremely hard on the less exemplary members of their own sex. In her novels Burney warns young women, either explicitly or by example, to have no social intercourse with women whose conduct is not beyond reproach. Burney's world is not one of moral values, but a struggle for social survival.

The sub-title of *Evelina*, which was published anonymously in 1778, was 'A Young Lady's Entrance into the World', and her heroine's name, a diminutive of Eve, must surely have been chosen deliberately. Milton's Eve was a favourite literary ideal of womanhood, often quoted in novels as the paradigm of the perfect wife, the ideal companion for man. At this period it was a literary model quoted by women writers entirely without irony, without the implication of innocence, that is, ignorance, riding for a Fall. Burney, in *Evelina*, does come very close to irony, since her Miltonic Eve is an *ingénue*, a sweet young thing coming out into society at the age of seventeen, learning to tread the tightrope of social conformity on the dangerous and thorny path between the safety of schoolroom and matrimony.

It is a short path, seven months in all, but it is full of pitfalls, trivial to the reader but highly serious to our heroine, for whom 'the world' means polite society. Burney, in the Preface, describes her heroine as 'young, artless, and inexperienced . . . the offspring of Nature', which certainly seems to echo Milton. Her doting but anxious guardian, Mr Villars, describes Evelina as 'innocent as an angel, and artless as purity itself', and readers of *Paradise Lost* know only too well that angels sometimes fall. Indeed, Evelina's secluded country upbringing is like a period in the Garden of Eden which has just come to an end as the story begins.

The letters of Evelina, by turns breathless, excited and abashed, are contrasted with the gravity and wisdom of her guardian, Mr Villars, whilst more worldly characters of mature years also give their views on Evelina's situation and at the same time carry the story forward with considerable adroitness and speed. The plot itself is of minimal importance, is reminiscent of Fielding, and is treated with a similar lightness of touch. Like Austen, Burney had been scribbling as a girl, and Evelina is the daughter of the heroine of a novel destroyed by Fanny Burney on her fifteenth birthday. Evelina's mother died when she was born, and her father has always refused to recognise her, which is why Mr Villars, once the guardian of her mother, has brought her up. The mystery surrounding her birth and her lack of respectable antecedents, to say nothing of the fortune from which her father's attitude has cut her off, is likely to impair her marriage prospects, and friends and relatives urge Mr Villars to take her father, Lord Belmont, to court. But Mr Villars does not favour a lawsuit, which would expose Evelina to unwelcome publicity 'repugnant to all female delicacy'. Finally a typical Burney character, the 'masculine' Mrs Selwyn, whom Burney portrays with typical ambiguity, since she behaves with more intelligence and real initiative than anyone else, but is described by Evelina herself as abrasive and lacking in femininity, resolves the situation by taking

Evelina to confront her father, who is overcome with emotion when he sees the girl's resemblance to her dead mother. It seems that, duped by a dishonest nursemaid who replaced the baby Evelina by her own child seventeen years ago, he has all this time been raising another child as his own. A simple solution to the mystery, and one which might have been guessed by any eighteenth-century reader. Evelina, meanwhile, has found a worthy suitor who loves her for herself alone; within days of signing herself Evelina Belmont for the first and last time she changes identity and surnames once more on becoming the wife of Lord Orville. Burney attached particular significance to a woman's change of name on marriage, as her next novel, *Cecilia*, showed; in *Cecilia* the patriarchal prejudice involved in the continuation of noble surnames was treated seriously and at length; in *Evelina* there is a deliciously light-hearted irony in the way the heroine is endowed with two noble surnames within a week, graced with the favour of first father and then husband.

But the real story of *Evelina* is the story of a young lady coming out into society and learning its rules. Although the world is a fairly silly one of balls, assemblies and tea-parties, it is a world fraught with hidden dangers and pitfalls for an inexperienced young woman. Evelina Anville, disowned by her father, in fact has no identity except as she appears in the eyes of others, and this is essentially the position of all young women when they 'come out' into the social world. Without the status conferred by men, they have and are nothing. Beauty is not enough. 'Remember, my dear Evelina,' writes her anxious guardian, 'nothing is so delicate as the reputation of a woman: it is, at once, the most beautiful and most brittle of all human things.'[1] Now that she has left the pastoral obscurity of her childhood, he warns her that she will need 'all the circumspection and prudence you can call to your aid . . . you must learn not only to *judge* but to *act* for yourself'.[2] This was to be the dominating theme for a whole school of women writers, including Austen, treated with varying degrees of seriousness. The *Bildungsroman* found a narrower female equivalent in the stories of young girls learning to cope with the social world on leaving the schoolroom, and making the correct choice of a mate.

Later Burney treated the theme with rather more heavy-handed seriousness, but her touch in *Evelina* is comparatively light-hearted and ironic. It is the work of a young woman for whom life is still fun, who has not yet become aware of sadness and tragedy, which would later overshadow her literary output. Her heroine is a quick learner in the ways of the world, for all her angelic innocence. She soon learns to respect gentility and look down her nose at the vulgar, particularly those who do not know their place. Forced to dine with a rather common family, she writes to Mr Villars: 'The dinner was ill-served, ill-cooked, and ill-managed. Had they been without *pretensions*, all this would have seemed of no consequence; but they aimed at appearing to advantage, and even fancied they succeeded.'[3] And when her vulgar maternal grandmother makes her accept an invitation to go to the Hampstead assembly with a mere Mr Smith, she writes: 'I was much chagrined at being thus compelled to owe even the shadow of an obligation to so forward a young man; but I determined that nothing should prevail upon me to dance with him, however my refusal might give offence.'[4] And this angel of goodness comments nastily on the fact that Mr Smith turned up 'dressed in a very showy manner, but without any taste, and the inelegant smartness of his air and deportment, his visible struggle, against education, to put on the fine gentleman'. Evelina's visible struggle, and one in which she ultimately succeeds, is away from her vulgar maternal and female relatives towards the aristocratic male connections represented by Lord Belmont and Lord Orville.

Evelina's attitude, priggish and snobbish, would be insufferable if it were not set against the fact that she is herself vulnerable in a world where a woman's reputation is the most brittle and perishable of all things, and where beauty invites danger as well as flattering attentions. Appearances can go against one, and for a woman in society appearance *is* reality. Forced to stay with a maternal grandmother who has no sense of the social niceties and is an unsuitable chaperone for a young lady, Evelina is constantly finding herself exposed in embarrassing public situations, and is seen by somebody, usually Lord Orville, the last person by whom she wants to be seen in a dubious light. Pleasure gardens were always to be a favourite venue for such public female embarrassment in Burney's novels, and *Evelina* is no exception. Taken to Vauxhall by the vulgar Branghton family, where the Branghton sisters behave in an immodest and unladylike fashion, Evelina writes: 'I must acknowledge, nothing could be more disagreeable to me, than being seen by Sir Clement Willoughby with a party at once so vulgar in themselves, and so familiar to me.'[5] Since Sir Clement had behaved with extreme impropriety to Evelina herself and shown himself no gentleman except in name this shame at being seen by him is particularly ironic, and highlights Evelina's awareness of her situation. She, as a young woman, is constantly at risk, while men like Sir Clement Willoughby can behave badly with impunity. But worse is to follow. At 'Mary-bone gardens' on a later occasion she finds herself separated from her party, is constantly accosted 'by some bold and unfeeling man to whom my distress . . . only furnished a pretence for impertinent witticisms, or free gallantry', and when she appeals for help to two ladies they turn out to be ladies of pleasure. And in this dreadful predicament she is seen by Lord Orville. 'I thought I should have fainted, so great was my emotion from shame, vexation, and a thousand other feelings.' The fact that 'he looked *greatly* concerned' was the only consolation 'for an evening the most painful of my life'. Her embarrassment and mortification reach a climax when Lord Orville, 'with an air of gravity that wounded my very soul' bids her good-night and asks for her address, so that he can call on her. 'O how I changed colour at this unexpected request! – yet what was the mortification I suffered, in answering, "My Lord, I am – in Holborn."'[6] Appearance is everything, and for Evelina the admission of such an unfashionable address is the final humiliation. But for the reader, conscious that Evelina has been in very real danger of ruining her life, this comic irony brings laughter not unmixed with relief.

Fanny Burney suffered all her life from the fact that the novel was 'a species of writing . . . never mentioned, even by its supporter, but with a look that fears contempt'.[7] Like Austen, she began scribbling early, but was ashamed of what she was doing:

> So early was I impressed myself with ideas that fastened degradation to this class of composition, that at the age of adolescence, I struggled against the propensity which, even in childhood, even from the moment I could hold a pen, had impelled me into its toils; and on my fifteenth birth-day, I made so resolute a conquest over an inclination at which I blushed, and that I had always kept a secret, that I committed to the flames whatever, up to that moment, I had committed to paper. And so enormous was the pile, that I thought it prudent to consume it in the garden.[8]

The eminent Dr Burney, who had only one novel in his library, a copy of Fielding's *Amelia*, a fact which helped to confirm her feelings of shame, knew nothing of this conflagration, and only her sister

Susanna 'wept, with tender partiality, over the imaginary ashes of Caroline Evelyn, the mother of Evelina'.

But she could not overcome her predilection. 'The passion . . . though resisted, was not annihilated' and *Evelina*, 'in defiance of every self-effort . . . struggled herself into life'. These quotations come from the dedication to her father of her last novel, *The Wanderer*, published in 1814, where she continues:

> If then, even in the season of youth, I felt ashamed of appearing to be a votary to a species of writing that by you, Sir, liberal as I knew you to be, I thought condemned; since your large library, of which I was then the principal librarian, contained only one work of that class; how much deeper must now be my blush . . . if the work which I here present to you, may not shew, in the observations which it contains . . . that an exteriour the most frivolous may enwrap illustrations of conduct, that the most rigid preceptor need not deem dangerous to entrust to his pupils.

And later still, in her *Memoirs of Doctor Burney*, published in 1832 when her father had long been dead and she was an old lady, she explained that she 'had written the little book, like unnumerable of its predecessors that she had burnt, simply for her private recreation. She had printed it for a frolic.'

But the frolic came to an end when her identity became known, and she was subdued by the burden of her fame, and the wish to please her father and his eminent circle of friends. She never again wrote a book with such a light touch as we find in *Evelina*, sentiment balanced by humour, the whole thing controlled by underlying irony. In all her novels, beginning with *Evelina*, Burney creates a host of minor characters who are quirky, often vulgar, and who owe a lot to the English tradition of theatrical comedy; funny, though sometimes not as amusing as they are intended to be, the sort of caricatures which Dickens would later make his own. But it is significant that Dr Burney liked these creations least of all in his daughter's first published work. He was disturbed by rough, crude characters, but particularly liked the moralising letters of the guardian, Mr Villars, and the characterisation of Lord Orville, a gentleman who is unfailingly correct in his behaviour, and who is little more than a walking stuffed shirt. After the anonymous publication of *Evelina*, Burney's work became both more sentimental and more self-consciously didactic. She struggled to avoid anything contentiously 'political', even though her later work shows a growing awareness of social injustice, and in her dedication of *The Wanderer* she expresses satisfaction in having won the approval of such different and differing men as Samuel Johnson and Edmund Burke. At one time, she claims, her first novel was 'the only subject upon which they met without contestation'.

In her life, too, Burney struggled to conform and appear in the correct company for the sake of her reputation, much as her heroines did. Burney, with no money of her own, dependent on the grace and favour of the Royal Family, first as Second Keeper of the Robes to Queen Charlotte, then as recipient of a royal pension and an author currying for favour, Burney also felt the brittle and all-important nature of a woman's reputation. In middle age she met Madame de Staël, and wrote enthusiastically to her father that she was 'a woman of the first abilities'. Dr Burney, in the role of masculine mentor so familiar from Burney novels, wrote to his daughter, asking her not to go and stay with her, as planned, because he had heard disturbing rumours about her political involvements, that she was a 'Diabolical Democrate' who had come to England to 'intrigue'. Upset at this information, Fanny defended de Staël as a woman very like herself, an '*idolising* Daughter' who 'from the best principles, those of filial reverence, entered into the opening of the Revolution just as her Father entered it', but goes on to assure her father: 'I would, nevertheless, give the world to avoid being a GUEST under their Roof, now I have heard even the shadow of such a Rumour'. And in a following letter: 'the Universe, now, would not induce me to go to poor Juniper, firmly as I believe it's unhappy Inhabitants cruelly calumniated, & truly worthy of every protection & support.' Whether from filial piety, a sense of her own vulnerability, or both, she was not prepared to give that support. She added: 'I have already done the painful task of writing my positive excuse to poor Me de Staël. I have not yet had an answer. I shall be deeply grieved if she is offended, but I see the *absolute Necessity* of the Measure.'[9] Just as her heroines are advised to avoid the company of women who read the wrong sort of books, whose heads have been turned by false notions, and whose behaviour does not conform to the conservative norm of female conduct, so female insecurity led Burney the writer to listen to her male mentor and avoid the company of a woman writer whom she instinctively began by liking and admiring, and found 'impossible to resist'. The fact that she was a good deal better informed about the political activities and motives of Necker and de Staël than her father was irrelevant, just as the essential innocence of non-conformist women in her novels is irrelevant to the issue. It is how they appear in the eyes of men like her father that matters.

Fanny Burney wrote long and entertaining letters to members of her family and to friends, and from time to time she also kept journals for the entertainment of her father and favourite sister, Susanna, so that the epistolary style came naturally to her, but like Edgeworth and Austen, she moved away from this form, and did not use it again after *Evelina*. Perhaps, for all of them, the form was already one which smacked too much of the past. But whilst Austen and Edgeworth gained greater authorial detachment by abandoning the epistolary form, Burney became less detached from her material when she adopted third person narrative, with dire results. Unlike Richardson, she used letters to introduce contrasting voices, which helped to distance her from her material, and controlled it. Also unlike Richardson, in her case the epistolary form made for brevity, which is unhappily lacking in her later work. And then she appears to have taken Dr Johnson's advice to her: 'Always aim at the eagle! – even though you expect but to reach a sparrow!'[10] Whilst Austen was content to go on painting her little bits of ivory, Burney became weighed down with a sense of social responsibility to her readers just because she was indulging in that despised literary form, the novel.

Cecilia appeared in 1782, four years after *Evelina*, and is a *Bildungsroman* on a much more ambitious scale than the first novel, in length as well as scope. *Cecilia*, like all her novels after *Evelina*, is in five volumes instead of three, and the scope of the heroine's adventures, temptations and general exposure to the world between leaving her country retreat for the first time and her inevitable end at the altar is much wider and much more serious, often bordering on the tragic. Although Burney still uses the central device of exposing her heroine to a series of social embarrassments, this time the difficulties are far from trivial, and are often a matter of life and death. To the modern reader the tone is steeped in sentimentality, the plot too often verges on melodrama. It is perhaps an inevitable result for a woman writer at that period, trying to keep within social conventions but determined to be sincere. Sentimentality is an alternative to irony; as for melodrama, it is the only way to stretch a heroine's plot at a time when young ladies simply did not have real-life adventures.

Dr Johnson's advice was bad, but then he was no artist. The trouble with aiming at an eagle instead of a sparrow is that if you miss the eagle you are liable to miss the sparrow as well. If Burney took his advice it was because he was another male mentor and she accepted the dominant opinion of the age that the novel was not an art form and could only be justified by its didactic content. Her justification of the novel in the dedication to *The Wanderer* closely resembles Dr Johnson's essay quoted in a previous chapter. The novel, she writes, 'points out the path of honour; and gives to juvenile credulity knowledge of the world, without ruin, or repentance; and the lessons of experience, without its tears'.

If Burney lacked the confidence to stick to what she could do best, to reject outside advice, and feel real pride in her art, it must also be said that she was a woman of wide human sympathies. A less knowing artist, less cunning, sharp and brittle than Austen, she was almost certainly a much nicer person. Under the veneer of self-protective conservatism was a woman painfully aware of human suffering and social injustice. It was for this reason that she chose, in *Cecilia*, a heroine who was also an heiress. For Burney this fact has implications which go far beyond the marriage market, though the heroine ultimately sacrifices her social responsibilities for love when she has to make a choice. In Cecilia we see virtue in action: though still under age when the story begins, she intends to use her money to relieve the distresses of the poor.

As always, the polarities in Burney are between youth and experience. Like Evelina, Cecilia is exposed to the world for the first time when she leaves her country retreat, her Garden of Eden, on the death of her guardian, and comes to London. She is an orphan, and Burney gives her three guardians who, in a somewhat schematic way, represent three vices. Mr Harrel, to whose protection and home she is first sent, is an extravagant man who lives beyond his means, causes distress to unpaid tradesmen, and tries to use Cecilia's wealth to get himself out of financial difficulties which end in suicide and ruin; her second guardian is a miser who thinks only of money and is a vulgar, comic character; whilst her third guardian, on whose protection she is forced to throw herself, is a proud snob who will not allow her to marry his son.

All Burney heroines are seen as very vulnerable in the world, which is dominated by men. Whilst Evelina is vulnerable through youth, beauty and inexperience, Cecilia's wealth renders her even more vulnerable. The older man whom she trusts most of all to give her fatherly advice is in fact scheming to marry her when his elderly wife dies, so that both his advice and protection are dangerous to her; her extravagant guardian uses her natural sympathy and his own position for his own gain and advancement, and succeeds in divesting her of a good deal of her inherited wealth; the miser sees her only as an asset, to be transferred in marriage to the highest bidder; while her third guardian, Mr Delvile, refuses to countenance a marriage to his only son because under the terms of a will her husband must change his surname to hers to perpetuate a deceased name. So, even as an heiress, Cecilia is only being used to perpetuate male vanity and pride.

By the end of the book Cecilia is penniless and very close to death. She has lost one half of her fortune through the extravagant Mr Harrel, and given away the other half in order to be able to marry Mortimer Delvile. Although the conventional message of women's novels was on the need for heroines to exercise self-control, in *Cecilia* it is the hero who drives the heroine to the brink of death by his passionate lack of it. He pines away, fights a duel which forces him to flee the country, persuades Cecilia (against her better judgement) to agree to a secret marriage which, to her public shame, is stopped at the altar by a mysterious stranger. She ends up penniless and alone, sick and raving in a humble room among strangers before the final rescue.

Austen took her title of 'Pride and Prejudice' from the final chapter of this novel, where heroine and author shriek out this phrase several times in capital letters, and the country doctor who has saved Cecilia's life condemns the custom of entangling estates and wills in order to perpetuate a surname after the male line has died out. Burney also intended to draw a distinction between false and true pride: Mr Delvile, who probably inspired Darcy more nearly than the hero, exemplifying false pride, while his wife, coming in a literary tradition of long-suffering wives, and not unlike the mother of Sir Charles Grandison, represents true pride. While Mr Delvile senior is cold and hostile, Cecilia finds in Mortimer's mother a sympathetic friend, a woman torn between family loyalty and the desire to see her son marry happily for love as she was not allowed to do in her youth. It is not only social convention but her respect for Mrs Delvile which makes Cecilia resist a clandestine marriage: 'She found, indeed, that it was not for nothing she was accused of pride, but she found at the same time so many excellent qualities, so much true dignity of mind, and so noble a spirit of liberality, that however great was the respect she seemed to demand, it was always inferior to what she was inclined to pay.'[11]

Delvile senior, like Darcy, is haughty and arrogant. No doubt it was from Mortimer Delvile's first proposal, by letter, and one which angers and offends the heroine, that Austen took more than a few hints for the first proposal that angered Elizabeth Bennet, and also the social analysis:

> My father, descended of a race which though decaying in wealth, is unsubdued in pride, considers himself as the guardian of the honour of his house . . . my mother, born of the same family, and bred to the same ideas, has strengthened this opinion by giving it the sanction of her own.
>
> Such being their sentiments, you will not, madam, be surprised that their only son, the sole inheritor of their fortune, and sole object of their expectations, should early have admitted the same. Indeed almost the first lesson I was taught was that of reverencing the family from which I was descended, and the name to which I am born. I was bid to consider myself as its only remaining support, and sedulously instructed neither to act nor think but with a view to its aggrandizement and dignity.
>
> Thus, unchecked by ourselves, and uncontrolled by the world, this haughty self-importance acquired by time a strength, and by mutual encouragement a firmness, which Miss Beverley alone could possibly, I believe, have shaken![12]

This analysis is only hinted at in *Pride and Prejudice*, but it is certainly there, and Elizabeth Bennet intends, after marriage, to cure him of his inbred faults. With the stiff reluctance which characterises the first proposal of Darcy, Mortimer Delvile goes on, in his letter, to confess that: 'This name which so vainly I have cherished and so painfully supported, I now find inadequate to recompense me for the sacrifice which its preservation requires.' Nevertheless it is Cecilia who has to make the sacrifice of her own estate to preserve his precious name. And with the renunciation of her estate all her plans for improving the conditions of her tenants have to be abandoned. There is no doubt, in either Cecilia's mind, or in that of the reader, that the greedy relative who cannot wait to get Cecilia out of her house when he learns of her marriage will not, as a landlord, be benevolent to the poor.

Having abandoned the shield of ironic ambiguity, Burney found herself in something of a dilemma, and one which comes out very clearly in *Cecilia*. She wanted to deal with real problems, and the real sufferings which life forces us to undergo. At the same time she was not prepared to challenge conservative values, at least not consciously. So her heroine, who starts out with so many good resolutions, and the capability of carrying them out, gives up her own autonomy and settles for conventional marriage. Burney would answer that no single woman can set herself against society and hope to be happy, something that all our fiction reading tends to confirm, even if individual case histories give us the opposite answer. Consciously she set out to distinguish between false and true pride; in fact she was writing about male patriarchal pride. In addition she shows us a world of greedy male predators, motivated by the lust for power and money, in which women, like the poor, are inevitable victims.

There is a gap of fourteen years between the publication of *Cecilia* and *Camilla*. Between 1782 and 1796 Burney had served and left the Royal Household, written rather unsuccessfully for the stage, married a penniless French refugee and given birth to a son at the advanced age of forty-two.

Her marriage had a radical effect on her attitude to writing. For the first time she saw it as a way of making a living, and there was at this time something of a division between women who wrote for money and those who did not need to. Indeed, when Mrs West published *A Gossip's Story* in 1797 she made a point, in her preface, of emphasising that she did not need to earn money from her work, being in possession of an annuity of £100 per annum, as though this information proved the purity of her didactic purpose, as well as her status as a lady.

The progress of Fanny Burney's courtship through her letters reads like one of her own novels, but it is doubtful whether she could have gone through with the marriage against such strong paternal opposition if it had not been for the possibility of earning through her writing. 'I have resources that I could bring forward to amend the little situation'[13] she wrote to her sister Susanna just before the troubled wedding, and Susanna answered: 'For my own part I can only say, & solicit, & urge to my Fanny to *print, print, print!* – Here is a resource – a certainty of removing present difficulties'.[14]

Burney wrote *Camilla* under financial pressure, a very different situation from the young woman who published her first novel as a frolic. In advertising the book to be sold by subscription, so that she and her family could earn the maximum, she wrote to a self-imposed deadline once the first advertisement appeared. She was torn between the need to make money and artistic integrity. On 6 July 1795 she wrote to her father: 'I will make my Work the best I can . . . I will neither be indolent, nor negligent, nor avaricious. I can never half answer the expectations that seem excited! I must try to forget them, or I shall be in a continual quivering.' But of course the most demanding and, for her, the most important expectations were always excited in her father, and on this occasion she was being less than frank. Only the day before she had written to her brother Charles: 'I am now going to work, very reluctantly, to *curtail my* plan, & obviate the threats of loss, or small profit.'[15]

The result of this pressure was a failed masterpiece, and she seems to have realised it, since she spent the rest of her long life, forty more years, revising and pruning it. A second edition appeared in 1802. From these two versions she finally concocted a third, which was finished in 1836 (by which time she was 84 years old) but which did not appear.

Apart from the pressure of writing to a deadline, something women novelists have never liked to do, there was the psychological pressure of pleasing her readers, of meeting the expectations of a public whose patronage she was now actively seeking, and which included such exalted readers as the Royal Household. Like all women writers of her period, she was already under pressure not to produce 'mere' novels but to aim for moral instruction. To this was added the pressure, because of her royal pension and the upper-class readership who was subscribing to the book, to be carefully conservative and avoid all contentious subjects. Anything that smacked of radicalism, even the liberal sympathies so obvious in *Cecilia*, was carefully excluded. As so often in her life, Burney was torn between her natural sympathies and the social pressure to conform, and the anxiety comes out in the Windsor journal she kept for her father when she stayed with the Royal Family just after the publication of *Camilla*. The book was dedicated to the Queen, and both the royal couple were gracious subscribers:

> 'There have been so many *bad* books published of that sort,' said Princess Mary, 'that every body should be glad of such a good one.' 'Yes,' said Princess Sophia, '& the Writers are all turned Democrats, they say.'

> I now explained that *Politics* were, *all ways*, left out: that once I had an idea of bringing in such as suited *me*, – but that, upon second thoughts, I returned to my more native opinion they were not a *feminine* subject for discussion, & that I even believed, should the little work sufficiently succeed to be at all generally read, it would be a better office to general Readers to carry them wide of all politics, to their domestic fire sides, than to open new matter of endless debate.[16]

Determined to please, Fanny Burney was clearly anxious to avoid even the suspicion of controversy in this book. Gone is the ironic ambiguity of *Evelina*, the mildly liberal sympathies of *Cecilia* which led her to suggest that personal wealth should be tempered by active benevolence towards the less fortunate. One can only guess what Burney meant by politics 'such as suited *me*', but from residual hints in the text I suspect that they were feminist rather than feminine. Odd comments here and there suggest that she had begun to question the role of women in society, and to see the part that society required them to play as a form of social conditioning rather than natural, and that she regarded this conditioning as both unjust and questionable. The very fact that she was now a mature woman helping to support a husband by her own efforts, and no longer a dependent daughter, must have forced her to that conclusion, even if the pressure of conformity and the need to earn a living prevented her from saying so outright. Those feelings were to come out much more clearly in her last novel.

Nevertheless, in spite of the way it was written and its inordinate length *Camilla* is a truly structured novel. Burney did not write a series of loosely connected episodes as a way out of her dilemma, as so many men have done in the same situation. She reassured her father on this point when she wrote to him on 6 July 1795:

> . . . it *is* of the same species as Evelina & Cecilia . . . more multifarious in the Characters it brings into action, – but all *wove*

into *one* . . . for so far is the Work from consisting of detached stories, that there is not, literally, one Episode in the whole plan.[17]

An interesting aspect of *Camilla* is the change of viewpoint necessitated by a woman of forty once more launching a seventeen-year-old heroine on to the world. Burney never did subscribe to the fashionable distinction between sense and sensibility so common to women writers of her period in quite the hard-line way that Edgeworth, Austen and Mrs West did, amongst others. Although she acknowledged that young women must learn to behave with judgement, she never thought that girls were capable of controlling their feelings through reason and prudence. This was asking too much of human nature, and her heroine Cecilia constantly blushes, faints, and weeps without being thought any the worse for giving way to her sensibility. Even in *Evelina* she had tended to see the world divided into the young and necessarily foolish on the one hand, and the older and wiser generation on the other, rather than making the division between prudence and passion. By the time she wrote *Camilla* she was convinced that there was an unbridgeable gulf between youth and experience, and this insight helped her to create a heroine who is a delight.

Camilla's virtues, 'a graceful simplicity, a disengaged openness, and a guileless freedom from affectation', though standard requirements for an acceptable heroine in courtship novels, have been transformed by Burney's mature eye into real qualities of youth. Gay, unaffected, young in temperament as well as years, she is remarkably free of the priggishness which tends to spoil our enjoyment of so many heroines of the period.

Since the full title of the novel is *Camilla, or A Picture of Youth*, Burney was clearly conscious of just what she was setting out to do, and she does not present her heroine in isolation, but as part of a whole group of young people in a family setting, unlike the orphaned Cecilia and pseudo-orphaned Evelina. One reason for the attractiveness of Camilla as a heroine is the fact that Burney avoided attributing any didacticism directly to her, and does not put moral messages in her young mouth. So, although Dr Burney could wax enthusiastic about *Camilla*, and claim that no other novel of his recollection could boast 'such good writing, thinking, & moral lessons', so that he thought it 'the best system of *Education*, I ever saw . . . apart from all its wit, humour, and entertainment',[18] the central character remains fresh and natural, a heroine very close in spirit to Tolstoy's Natasha before she was so transformed by marriage.

Camilla is impetuous, but this is because she is young, and not because she is weak of intellect or rebellious. It is a much more natural portrayal of girlhood than the conventional wisdom of the didactic novel normally allowed for, with its positive emphasis on the need for prudence, judgement, and rigid self-control. This was a result of Burney's mature reflection, and not simply a happy accident. In the years before she began to work in earnest on the novel she jotted down: 'It is a mistake to suppose the intellect weak in youth, because the judgment is erroneous.' And on another occasion she noted: 'Precaution is not natural in youth, whose greatest [danger] because greatest weakness is confidence in its first impulse, which is commonly pleasant because kind. To be just requires more reflexion; to have foresight, demands more experience.'

Camilla also reminds one of Tolstoy's Natasha because she is set firmly and convincingly against a family background. By the standards of the novel, including Burney's own previous work, her background is refreshingly normal. She has parents, brothers and sisters, and a doting uncle, and the social setting is that of the country gentry. Her uncle is wealthy, her father, a clergyman, is not, and Camilla's expectations are as near average as Burney can make them, a far cry from Evelina, the disowned daughter of a lord and Cecilia, the heiress. Burney's previous heroines have their origins in the novel rather than observed experience, but Camilla is firmly rooted in reality.

Like Burney's previous heroines, Camilla is put through a series of embarrassing situations, some with truly serious implications, as in *Cecilia*, some rather trivial and to do with social propriety, as in *Evelina*. But as in *Evelina*, these trivial occasions are serious because the heroine is seen by the man she loves. Whilst Orville is mature enough not to misjudge Evelina because of the situation in which he sees her, Edgar Mandlebert, himself rather young and under the influence of a misogynistic tutor, condemns Camilla in consequence and decides, for a time, that she would be an unsuitable wife.

Because of Burney's underlying attitudes and a new realism which makes Camilla's supposed misdemeanours natural, understandable and even likeable, Edgar, tutor, mentor and husband to be, stands out as an insufferable prig. As so often in Burney, her conventional

morality is at odds with her true feelings. Edgar's attitudes are to
some extent explained by the influence of his tutor, and his own
youth, even though they embody all the conventional expectations of
Cœlebs in search of a wife. Meanwhile the reader is struck by the
contrast between the behaviour of the young women in the story, with
the utter licence allowed to young men. Camilla's greatest crime is
that she cannot manage her pin money when she leaves home for the
first time. One of the reasons she gets into debt is that her brother
Lionel, a student at Oxford, had played on her feelings and got most
of her pin money from her. Lionel, who has been using his privileged
position at Oxford to gamble and commit adultery, goes on to send
anonymous threatening letters to his uncle in order to extort more
money to pay his debts. Clermont, another young man of the family,
incurs debts abroad during his grand tour. Burney never points an
authorial finger at the contrast between the male licence and female
restriction she is describing, and the reader is left to draw his or her
own conclusions, which are inescapable: compared with most young
men, most young women appear not only good, but positively saint-
like. Thus Burney avoids contentious politics, but nevertheless gets
her views across.

There is ambiguity even in the set sermon which, to the delight of
Dr Burney, Mr Tyrold preaches to his daughter Camilla in a letter:

The temporal destiny of women is enwrapt in still more
impenetrable obscurity than that of man. She begins her career by
being involved in all the worldly accidents of a parent; she
continues it by being associated in all that may environ a husband.

Mr Tyrold goes on to preach against imprudence and impatience in
the approved fashion:

Good sense will shew you the power of self-conquest and point to its
means. It will instruct you to curb those unguarded movements
which lay you open to the strictures of others. It will talk to you of
those boundaries which custom forbids your sex to pass.

The fact that Burney uses the word 'custom' is significant, and
Camilla's father goes on: 'The proper education of a female, either
for use or for happiness, is still to seek, still a problem beyond human
solution'.[19] This is light years away from the usual certainties of the
didactic courtship novel.

The young women portrayed in this novel are judged in terms of their innate characteristics rather than their overt behaviour. We are shown the beautiful Indiana as vain and empty-headed by nature, rather than behaving with vanity to prove a point. And for once the question of conventional female conduct is treated not as an immutable law which women break at their peril, but as a boundary set by men. Seen at the theatre by Edgar, apparently unchaperoned, the authorial voice comments:

> Camilla now began to regret she had not accompanied Mrs Arlbery. She had thought only of the play and its entertainment, till the sight of Mandlebert told her that her situation was improper; and the idea only occurred to her by considering that it would occur to him.[20]

The fact that women were judged by appearances was always a dominant theme in Burney's novels. Treated with amused irony in *Evelina* and with total seriousness in *Cecilia*, in *Camilla* she began to question the justice and value of such a custom, whilst in *The Wanderer* she condemned it outright.

Mrs Arlbery, like Mrs Selwyn in *Evelina*, is another one of those 'masculine' emancipated women that Burney loved to invent, imbued with much life and authority, but at the same time made the subject of enough criticism on the part of other fictional characters to allow it to appear that Burney is following convention in condemning such women, though in fact she is doing nothing of the sort. Thus, Evelina describes Mrs Selwyn:

> Mrs Selwyn is very kind and attentive to me. She is extremely clever; her understanding, indeed, may be called *masculine*; but, unfortunately, her manners deserve the same epithet; for, in studying to acquire the knowledge of the other sex, she has lost all the softness of her own . . . I have never been personally hurt at her want of gentleness; a virtue which, nevertheless seems so essential a part of the female character, that I find myself more awkward, and less at ease, with a woman who wants it, than I do with a man. She is not a favourite with Mr Villars, who has often been disgusted at her unmerciful propensity to satire.[21]

It is highly doubtful whether Mr Villars, even though in the novel he is the exponent of so much conventional wisdom, would have approved of his creator, with *her* propensity for satire. This ambiguity allows Burney to reflect conventional attitudes, appear to condone them, while an alternative reading is open to any reader of slightly more than average intelligence. Mrs Selwyn commands respect: within days of taking charge of Evelina she manages to get the girl accepted by her father with a minimum of fuss, something that Mr Villars has failed to do in seventeen years, by the simple expedient of taking the girl to see him and speaking bluntly.

Mrs Arlbery (and her name bears a suspicious resemblance to the married name of her creator) is a witty and sophisticated woman of the world who defies the conventions, and neither Camilla nor the reader can help liking her for her honesty and intelligence. Edgar considers her a most unsuitable companion for Camilla, though Camilla enjoys her company and, since Edgar, like Mr Villars, represents the conventional proprieties the conventional reader can feel reassured and safely pass the book on to vulnerable young ladies in his or her charge. But Mrs Arlbery also condemns Edgar for his narrow ideas and the expectations of conduct in a wife which he holds, and she calls him a 'watcher', a condemnatory epithet which fits in well with Burney's ever-recurring theme of women being judged solely by appearances.

Camilla has many faults. It is far too long, and Burney easily lapses into a high-flown sentimentality augmented by a verbosity and choice of phrase which is less than happy. But in the ambition of its structure, its truthful depiction of English country life, and the range and insight shown in the portrayal of character, it represents a milestone in the development of the English novel. Social pressure made Fanny Burney into a moralist when she was by instinct a realist, and her gift for evoking real people in scenes which feel true to life is most fully developed in *Camilla*. Unlike Tolstoy's Natasha, we do not see what marriage to Edgar will do to the joyous spirit of the delightful Camilla, but like her previous heroine Cecilia, Burney's Camilla is, by the end of the book, worn down by her experience of the world. And whilst Cecilia was a victim of a predatory male world, Camilla is the victim of the social conditioning which that male world imposes. So Burney writes of her heroine: 'Whatever she had personally to bear, she constantly imagined some imprudence or impropriety had provoked.' Once safely married and under the tutelage of Edgar, we are told, happiness gave her 'a gaiety no longer to be feared'. In spite of the conventional ending Burney emphasises once more that the difficulties of her young couple were due 'to the natural heedlessness of youth unguided' and in the case of Edgar 'to the acquired distrust of experience that had been wounded', that is, the influence of his embittered and misogynistic tutor. Though Edgar, the 'watcher', the male mentor, tutor and future husband, such a familiar figure in women's courtship novels (Mr Knightley is perhaps the most famous example), is allowed to voice all the conventional wisdom on female conduct, Burney makes it clear that he is wrong to behave as he does, and should not have judged Camilla wholly on appearances.

In all her novels the importance of appearances to a woman moving in a social world was a dominant theme, and in her last novel Burney took this theme to its furthest extreme. *The Wanderer* was published in 1814, two years after she had returned from a ten-year exile in France brought about by the renewal of the war with England, and her heroine is a mysterious woman fleeing to England during the time of Robespierre. When she appears in the first chapter to beg to be taken on board a boat full of English people also making their escape, everything but her sex is in doubt: her age, class, nationality, and even race, since she has darkened her skin and put on a heavy disguise. Later in the story she is revealed as young and beautiful, but she refuses to divulge her name or give any account of her background.

The ultimate dénouement is conventional enough, but Burney's initial device is interesting because it allows her to develop, more fully than ever before, her idea that women are judged wholly by appearances and are victims of society as a result. The fact that the heroine is alone and unprotected, and that her background is a mystery, lays her open to very bad treatment. Women exploit or snub her, men lay siege to her honour. Those, on the other hand, who first see her in a drawing room without knowing anything of the mystery which surrounds her, are ready to admire her and take her into their houses, until they find out the truth, whereupon they cannot turn her out fast enough.

But there is also another, new, theme in this novel, which Burney had not tackled before, and which was just beginning to occupy the minds of women novelists, and that was the problem a woman of breeding and education faces when she is unexpectedly forced to earn her own living. It is a dominant theme in Mary Brunton's *Self-*

Control, published in 1812, and even Jane Austen touched on the problem in her portrayal of Jane Fairfax in *Emma* four years later. It was a theme that was to grow in importance throughout the century, and Charlotte Brontë, in particular, gave it passionate voice.

For the author of *Evelina, Cecilia* and *Camilla* to create a heroine who is reduced to giving music lessons and doing plain sewing to try and keep herself is something of a one-woman revolution in itself, and shows to what extent age and experience had changed Fanny Burney. This is no longer the voice of Dr Burney's young daughter viewing the world with fond amusement from the safety of the drawing room, but the voice of an ageing woman who had experienced sickness, poverty and war, and who knew from personal experience that life required more of a woman, if she was to survive, than delicacy and decorum.

The heroine of *The Wanderer* is ill-equipped to support herself, as she is the first to admit, and literary convention ultimately returns her to the safety of fortune, marriage, and aristocratic relations. But not before certain points have been made:

> How few, she cried, how circumscribed, are the attainments of women! and how much fewer and more circumscribed still, are those which may in their consequences, be useful as well as ornamental, to the higher, or educated class! those through which, in the reverses of fortune, a FEMALE may reap benefit without abasement.[22]

The heroine soon comes to feel that the ability to earn an independent living is preferable to charity, and the 'helplessness to resist any species of indignity' to which we see her exposed. Returning to a theme in *Cecilia*, Burney also shows how upper-class people make the lot of the poor worse by failing to pay them what they owe. Having given music lessons to fashionable young ladies, the heroine finds it impossible to get her accounts settled.

The theme of fortitude, which runs through many women's novels of the period, from Mary Brunton's *Self-Control* to Mrs Radcliffe's *Mysteries of Udolpho*, published twenty years earlier, also makes its appearance in *The Wanderer*, showing how far Burney had moved in her view of the world as a safe and stable place. The unknown heroine reads a letter from an unknown guardian or friend:

In your present lonely, unprotected, unexampled situation, many and severe may be your trials . . . chiefly bear in mind, what has been the principle of your education, and what I wish to be that of your conduct and character through life: That where occasion calls for female exertion, mental strength must combat bodily weakness; and intellectual vigour must supply the inherent deficiencies of personal courage; and that those, only, are fitted for the vicissitudes of human fortune, who, whether male or female, learn to suffice to themselves. Be this the motto of your story.[23]

The heroine of *The Wanderer* has neither guardian nor male mentor to look after her, and though many characters in the book offer her charity, this only brings its own embarrassments. Essentially, she is alone, and has to fend for herself, and the story only goes to prove that women of her class are not equipped to do so. The sub-title is *Female Difficulties*, and we are left in no doubt as to what these are: 'How insufficient, she exclaimed, is a FEMALE to herself! How utterly dependent upon situation – connexions – circumstance!' And she goes on: 'Appearances are against me'.[24]

In earlier novels Burney had emphasised that women are judged by appearances and must take care not to show themselves in compromising situations, however innocent their intentions. In this last novel she shifts the emphasis to complain of humanity's lack of trust, mainly through the words of the hero who, alone, sees the heroine for what she really is and comments on the cruelty and hypocrisy of society. Typically, Burney leaves it to the wild Elinor, condemned for revolutionary and irreligious ideas, to voice overt feminist sentiments, but the practical experience of the heroine leads her to voice sentiments which come close enough to the same conclusion: 'What is woman, – with the most upright designs, the most rigid circumspection, – what is woman unprotected? She is pronounced upon only from outward semblance . . . . [25]

5. The Gothic Alternative

IN the last chapter we have seen how Fanny Burney was torn between her natural instincts and the social pressure to conformity. For the woman novelist who did not write for a living there was the emotional pressure of her family and friends, whilst the professional writer had to contend with market forces, which favoured conservative attitudes in dealing with the position of women. Of course, even the amateur 'lady' writer was unlikely to see her work in print if her work represented a radical departure from prevailing attitudes.

In addition to these social pressures on women writers we also have to consider the restriction imposed by the imagination itself. Most novelists, most writers, are concerned with showing the world as it is, not as it might or ought to be; the tendency towards conservatism which can be noted in most great writing of the past is due to this fact. Good writers are concerned with truth, and truth compels the writer to tell it how it is, not how he or she would like it to be. Visionary writers are a comparative rarity. The language of the novel at this period gave women very little scope for an alternative vision of female destiny.

During the eighteenth century there were only two basic plots for heroines. There was the story with the happy ending – the comic courtship plot with its emphasis on conduct; and the story with the unhappy ending, that of seduction, abduction and ruin. The latter variety tended to be disapproved of by the moral guardians of young ladies who frowned on the habit of novel-reading, and could only be justified on didactic grounds. Women novelists, so uneasy about their occupation, tended to stick to the safer ground of the comic courtship novel with a happy ending, often contrasting the exemplary conduct of their heroine by having a sub-plot in which a young woman is brought to ruin and disgrace by some variation of the second plot.

If the comic plot can be labelled the Grandison story, and the tragic one Clarissa, there is a third, hybrid archetypal plot which could aptly be called the Pamela plot. This is the story of the woman who is a victim of male abduction but through personal initiative and fortitude wins through to a happy ending of respectable marriage, usually with a fortune thrown in. This was a basic plot which women novelists, particularly the more popular ones, did seize on and develop. It offered more scope for a story full of adventure and incident than the courtship novel with its emphasis on social propriety. For professional women writers aiming at a wider market it had the added attraction of allowing them to portray women in situations which required them to be self-reliant and courageous without outraging social convention, since their heroines were the victims of wicked males. Fanny Burney made a gradual switch from dependent lady to independent professional woman, and we saw how this affected the tone of her novels. For a woman like Charlotte Smith, starting her career as a novelist in order to support herself after an unsatisfactory marriage, a heroine who was forced by circumstances to take charge of her own destiny and act on her own initiative had obvious attractions. It was a story-line that provided a viable female alternative to the male picaresque, as long as certain constraints were observed: the heroine must not lose her virtue, and must act in an unconventional manner only under duress. The elaboration of suitable adventures for such a heroine, that is, of dangers which left the heroine essentially unscathed, being rooted in fantasy rather than reality, led to the development of the Gothic mode. And the Gothic mode eventually became an imaginative vehicle for feminism, since it provided a radical alternative to the daylight reality of conformity and acceptance, offering a dark world of the psyche in which women were the imprisoned victims of men.

We can see the problem involved in presenting a radical alternative through fiction in the work of Mary Wollstonecraft. She was not, admittedly, a born novelist, and would probably never have tried her hand at the form if it had not been considered the most obvious one for women of her era to attempt. Her first novel, *Mary,* was published in 1788, the same year that saw the publication of Charlotte Smith's *Emmeline.* Wollstonecraft's novel is a disastrous attempt at radical realism, an autobiographical novel which attempts to show a heroine trying to live by different tenets from the conventional ones, but it is unconvincing and, one suspects, unconvinced. *Emmeline*, on the other hand, is a rattling romantic yarn on the Pamela model. The heroine resists seduction, abduction and the bullying of rich and powerful males through a series of adventures, some with Gothic overtones which inspired Mrs Radcliffe. But at the time of her death in 1797, three years after the publication of *Udolpho* and nearly a decade after she first read *Emmeline* and reviewed it in disapproving tones,[1] Mary Wollstonecraft was herself using the Gothic mode to write a protest novel, one which showed far more imaginative power than the more realistic *Mary*.

In *Mary* the central figure is given all the rhapsodic emotions which more conservative women novelists tried so consistently to discourage, and considered dangerous for personal survival: 'Sensibility is the most exquisite feeling of which the human soul is susceptible: when it pervades us, we feel happy . . .. It is this quickness, this delicacy of feeling, which enables us to relish the sublime touches of the poet, and the painter . . .'[2] But it is in action, not sentiment, that the novel reader will find a prescription for reality, and the plot of *Mary* is unspeakably lame, in fact it confirms the warnings of conservative novelists that unconventional ideas and a romantic sensibility will do a heroine nothing but harm. Forced into a loveless marriage at an early age, Mary, like Wollstonecraft, travels to Lisbon to nurse a dying friend. There the heroine meets her true soulmate, a sickly man called Henry. She protests against her married state and asks herself:

> . . . have I desires implanted in me only to make me miserable? Will they never be gratified? . . . With these notions can I conform to the maxims of worldly wisdom? Can I listen to the cold dictates of worldly prudence, and bid my tumultous passions cease to vex me . . .?[3]

Unfortunately the answer offered by the author to these rhetorical questions in terms of plot are yes, these desires are implanted only to plague, no, they will not be gratified, yes, our heroine can and will conform to worldly wisdom, and will also listen to the cold dictates of wordly prudence, which leaves the conservative novelists of sense and prudence clear victors of the field. Although Mary returns from Lisbon determined not to live with her husband ('I will work,' she cried, 'do any thing rather than be a slave') her resolutions come to nothing. Henry dies, Mary agrees to live with her husband, but his touch fills her with disgust, she suffers from poor health, travels a good deal, throws herself into good works, and seems destined for an early grave. It is decidedly an evasion, with the heroine avoiding both the indignities of adultery and plain sewing.

Since Mary Wollstonecraft was herself to live with a man who was not her husband it is unlikely that she was prevented by personal prudery from giving a different ending to her story, though consideration for the reactions of her readers might have been an inhibiting factor. But my over-riding feeling is that for Wollstonecraft, who was not a novelist of originality and genius, there simply were no satisfactory literary models for her to draw on. Having created a heroine trapped in a conventional morality but emotionally at odds with it, there was nowhere for her fictional Mary to go, and she simply stagnates within her situation instead of changing it. At the same time Wollstonecraft clearly felt that to concoct a happy fictional ending would be a falsehood. Real life did not provide women with contrived endings. In real life women stayed imprisoned in their situation.

No doubt it was this latter consideration which prompted her to criticise Charlotte Smith's *Emmeline* when she reviewed it anonymously in the *Analytical Review* in July 1788: 'The false expectations these wild scenes excite, tend to debauch the mind, and throw an insipid kind of uniformity over the moderate and rational prospects of life', she wrote, but the end result is to make her critical voice indistinguishable from that of her most conservative sisters, who always aimed to make their young women readers realise that their prospects were severely limited and that marriage was the doorway to duty and responsibility, not freedom and romance.

The fact is that, for all her radical ideals, Wollstonecraft had no alternative reality to offer her readers, or through which she could propel her heroine. Within the realistic mode she was as fettered as Burney or Austen, and it was only through fantasy that any alternative, or some form of escape, was possible. Of course, unlike more conservative women novelists, she tended to have a clearer understanding of cause and effect. Writing of Mary's mother at the beginning of the book, she says:

> As she was sometimes obliged to be alone . . . she sent to the metropolis for all the new publications, and while she was dressing her hair, and she could turn her eyes from the glass, she ran over those most delightful substitutes for bodily dissipation, novels.'[4]

At one level this is the conventional indictment of novel-reading, but Wollstonecraft is unusual in seeing why women become addicted to fiction – as a substitute for the life they cannot live.

Whatever their personal life styles or conscious political ideas, the fact is that at this period there was very little difference in attitude between the Jacobin and anti-Jacobin stance as far as women's fiction is concerned. For any writer aiming at realism, reality proved too strong a fetter. In addition, radical women who were interested in revolutionary ideas, as Wollstonecraft was, found precious little in radical male ideology to change the image of woman. It was precisely because of this blind side in her idol Rousseau that Wollstonecraft was stirred into writing her *Vindication of the Rights of Woman*.

In 1791, three years after Wollstonecraft's rather lame first venture into fiction, the actress Mrs Inchbald, a friend of William Godwin, from whom she apparently received literary advice, published *A Simple Story*, a novel which enjoyed both critical and popular success, and was much admired by Edgeworth.[5] Mrs Inchbald undoubtedly led an unconventional life, she moved in radical circles, but her novel purveys all the conventional wisdom meted out to young women by the most staunch supporters of Burke. So the heroine of the first half of the book, Miss Milner, is brought to a bad end by her own lack of prudence and self-control:

> From her infancy she had been indulged in all her wishes to the extreme of folly, and habitually started at the unpleasant voice of control – she was beautiful, she had been too frequently told the high value of that beauty, and thought those moments passed in wasteful idleness during which she was not gaining some new conquest – she had besides a quick sensibility, which too frequently discovered itself in the immediate resentment of injury or neglect – she had acquired also the dangerous character of a wit.[6]

Even if one makes allowances for the author's desire to maximise her profits from writing, one feels she might have taken a slightly less hard line, and at least allowed her a little wit. In the second half of the book her daughter Matilda, in sharp contrast to her dead mother, is a model of female virtues, quiet and submissive. She never blames her father for his cruel rejection, and when she is abducted, rescued by her father, and taken to his bosom, she behaves in the approved manner: 'she feared to speak, or clasp him in return for his embrace, but falling on her knees clung round his legs, and bathed his feet with her tears.'[7] The situation of Matilda is not unlike that of Evelina, except that it is treated quite without irony, and in conclusion the reader is told that she:

> has beheld the pernicious effects of an improper education in the destiny which attended the unthinking Miss Milner – on the opposite side, then, what may not be hoped from that school of prudence – though of adversity – in which Matilda was bred?

It needs a very careful eye to detect much difference of outlook between Mrs Inchbald and some of her conservative contemporaries. She does tend to show her characters in the grip of overpowering emotions which they are quite unable to control, whereas novelists of 'sense' like Austen, West and Edgeworth tend to assume that it is always possible to control emotions which reason and judgement teach us to overcome. But in the process she also seems to be undermining the little autonomy which women could claim. Burney's depiction of heroines who feel, love and suffer but nevertheless learn to cope satisfactorily with the conflict between interior feelings and exterior reality without falling a victim to either in the long run seems both less simplistic and more constructive.

But in order to escape the restrictions imposed on a woman of good family it was necessary to escape into a world, not just of romance, but of fantasy. Fantasy not only gave scope to the imagination, but made it possible for a heroine to act on her own initiative, to show positive rather than negative virtues. As we shall see, it is characteristic of Mrs Radcliffe's Gothic mode to he highly artificial, that is, the reader is constantly aware of being involved in a charade of make-believe. This was an important factor for a society that believed in keeping its daughters pure in thought, word and deed.

Women writers became increasingly concerned to promote positive virtues in their women readers. They soon became dissatisfied with preaching merely prudence and propriety, the conduct of courtship. The Gothic novel not only unleashed the imagination, but made it possible to show women acting boldly on their own behalf, with fortitude and courage. In this sense the Gothic novel was itself only a link in the chain, since it was followed by more realistic novels showing young women coping with adversity and disaster. Mary Brunton's *Self-Control*, published in 1812, which shows a heroine coping with the death of a parent, poverty, and the unscrupulous machinations of a seducer in a realistic English setting, has many links with *Udolpho*, published eighteen years earlier.

Emmeline, or *The Orphan of the Castle*, provides an earlier link in the chain of development. Published six years after Burney's *Cecilia* it has many resemblances to the earlier novel, whilst introducing a number of mildly Gothic scenes at the beginning and end of the main narrative which are thought to have inspired Mrs Radcliffe, whose *Mysteries of Udolpho* appeared six years after the publication of Charlotte Smith's novel. For the modern reader it has the additional interest of occasional sharp jabs of feminist sarcasm which are particularly refreshing after the conventional sentimentality of Burney.

At the beginning of the novel the heroine is a young girl living alone with a housekeeper in a remote and dilapidated castle, an orphan ignored and neglected by her aristocratic relatives because she is presumed to be illegitimate. At the age of sixteen her life changes when the housekeeper dies. Emmeline, like Mrs Radcliffe's Emily a few years later, has to cope with death:

> In strong and excellent understandings there is, in every period of life, a force which distress enables them to exert, and which prevents their sinking under the pressure of those evils which overwhelm and subdue minds more feeble and unequal.
>
> The spirits of Emmeline were yet unbroken by affliction, and her understanding was of the first rank . . . . Instead therefore of giving way to tears and exclamations, she considered how she should best perform all she now could do for her deceased friend . . . .[8]

This is a very different note from the trivial social embarrassments of young Evelina, and one which was to be increasingly heard in women's fiction. Radcliffe's Emily would have to cope with the physical reality of death more than once, with the death of her father and later of her aunt, whilst the two women are imprisoned in the castle; Mary Brunton's Laura lays out her father's corpse without shrinking. But with death goes the fear of an overwrought imagination, also to be exploited by Mrs Radcliffe: that night Emmeline 'started from her imperfect slumber, and fancied she heard the voice of Mrs Carey calling on her for help! – which the stillness of the night, interrupted only by the cries of the owls which haunted the ruins, added to the gloomy and mournful sensations of her mind'.

Emmeline is the only child of a first son and heir, but since she is supposed to have been born out of wedlock her father's estate has been inherited by his younger brother, Emmeline's uncle, Lord Montreville, who neglects her shamefully. But Lord Montreville has an only son, Delamere, who falls passionately in love with Emmeline during a visit to the remote castle where she has been brought up in isolation. Delamere, ardent and impetuous, is clearly modelled on Delvile in Burney's *Cecilia*, and there is also a clear similarity in the family conflicts which ensue. Lord Montreville is sternly opposed to the marriage, and tends to punish Emmeline for his son's behaviour, which is doubly unjust, since Emmeline does not love Delamere. When she finally agrees to an engagement it is only to humour this wild and impetuous man, and prevent a possible tragedy.

Although the message of the conventional courtship novel was the need for women to control their passions, in *Emmeline*, as in *Cecilia*, it is the hero who is quite incapable of controlling his emotions. But Charlotte Smith is more critical of such behaviour than Burney, who tends to excuse it, while Smith sees it as the result of the indulgent upbringing accorded to young men, particularly to the son and heir of a wealthy family:

> Accustomed from his infancy to the most boundless indulgences, he never formed a wish the gratification of which he expected to be denied: and if such a disappointment happened, he gave way to an impetuosity of disposition that he had never been taught to restrain . . .. He was generous, candid, and humane; and possessed many other good qualities, but the defects of his education had obscured them.[9]

Emmeline shows many instances of Charlotte Smith's capacity to criticise the male-dominated society in which she lived, but her ability to portray male behaviour as the result of an education geared to patriarchal privilege (instead of concentrating exclusively on the problems of female conduct and misconduct within that accepted patriarchal framework) was something new, and represented an important step forward in women's fiction. Burney herself was influenced by it. In her subsequent novel *Camilla* she contrasts the demure goodness of the young women in her story with the unlicensed wildness of young men at the same age. Later novelists, particularly Charlotte and Anne Brontë, were increasingly outspoken on the damaging indulgence meted out to sons in order to 'make a man' of them.

We get a further foretaste of high Gothic when Emmeline, during Delamere's first visit to the castle, is terrified on hearing rustling noises after dark. Delamere bursts into the room and pours out 'incoherent expressions of frantic passion'; Emmeline tries to escape by running through the gloomy passages of the castle, and eventually succeeds in getting away, since she knows the lay-out of the castle and he does not. But it is Emmeline who is forced by her uncle to leave the castle, to avoid a misalliance which she does not even desire. She spends a good deal of the rest of the novel being pursued by the passionate Delamere, and trying to avoid his attentions. When, at one stage, she agrees to marry him if he promises to stay away from her for a year, her motive is not ambition or love, but kindness and affection.

Like *Cecilia, Emmeline* is also about misguided pride and its tragic consequences. Both Delamere's parents are strongly opposed to the marriage, and Lord Montreville puts great pressure on his niece to try and prevent the marriage: he threatens to leave her penniless, and tries to arrange a marriage for her, but young Emmeline is shown to have inner resources of true pride and dignity which enable her to resist both Delamere's selfish passion and his father's high-handed arrogance. When an emissary from her uncle informs her that she must marry an elderly man or be left quite penniless, she is told that:

> there *can* be no reason, indeed none will be allowed, or listened to, or heard of, why you should not eagerly, and instantly, and joyfully accept a proposal so infinitely superior to what you have any claim, or right, or pretence to . . .[10]

there is a tone of playful irony which looks forward to *Pride and Prejudice* and the high-handed proposals of Collins and Darcy, rather than back to the pompous solemnity of Mortimer Delvile's first proposal in *Cecilia*. Charlotte Smith makes her heroine refuse the proposal 'with a firmness of voice and manner which resentment, as well as noble pride supplied' and walks out of the room:

> leaving the unsuccessful ambassador astonished at that strength of mind, and dignity of manner, which he did not expect in so young

a woman, and somewhat mortified, that his masculine eloquence, on which he was accustomed to pride himself, and which he thought generally unanswerable, had so entirely fallen short of the effect he expected.

This is as sharp as anything Austen was to publish later, and the target of her irony was far more obvious. Charlotte Smith did not go in for veiled ambiguity or subtle, concealed irony. Her sarcasm was overt and she was not, like Burney, an apologist for the status quo.

Charlotte Smith, who had previously published poetry, wrote *Emmeline* shortly after leaving her husband, and she was criticised after its publication for giving an unfavourable portrait of her husband in the book. It is possible that her experience of marriage to a man who constantly got into debt had not enhanced her view of man as woman's superior, protector and provider, and helped to sharpen her pen. While she needed to write a popular novel in order to support herself, there is a strain of acidity in the book which is both refreshing and new. For instance, her highly ironic portrait of Miss Galton, an old maid, is not only something new in itself, but is used very effectively to highlight a male-dominated society where the chief function of women is to feed male vanity:

> Miss Galton, who by long dependance and repeated disappointments had acquired the qualifications necessary for a patient hearer, acquiesced in smiling silence to all his assertions; looked amazed in the right place; and heard, with great complacency, his wonderful success at cards, and the favour he was in with women of the first fashion at spa.[11]

A little after this we are told about 'Miss Galton, who being neither young, handsome, or rich, had been left to go out alone'. It has been suggested that Austen's gibes at ideal heroines in *Northanger Abbey* were prompted by her reading of *Emmeline*, though Mrs Radcliffe's Emily could just as well have prompted them. On balance, it is more likely that Smith had a positive influence. Miss Galton foreshadows those older women, the old maids without looks, status or fortune whom Austen was to portray so well as the forgotten dimension of a woman's lot.

Whilst Burney, in *Cecilia*, anxious to avoid being thought a diabolical democrat, aimed at compromise by making a distinction between false and true pride, Charlotte Smith is much more

trenchant in her condemnation of the overruling arrogance of the
aristocracy. Mrs Delvile sympathised with Cecilia, at least, even if
she upheld her husband's stand, but Lady Montreville is even more
arrogant than her husband in her hostility to the heroine:

> She lamented, whenever she deigned to speak of her, that the laws
> of this country, unlike those of better regulated kingdoms, did not
> give people of fashion power to remove effectually those who
> interfered with their happiness, or were inimical to their views. 'If
> this little wretch,' said she, 'was in France, it would not be difficult
> to put an end to the trouble she has dared to give us. A *lettre de cachet*
> would cure the creature of her presumption, and place her where
> her art and affectation should not disturb the peace of families of
> high rank.'[12]

Since *Emmeline* was published in 1788, just before the French
Revolution, the reference to French methods of dealing with those
who cause difficulties to people of fashion has an ominously prophetic
tone which was probably unintentional. The high-handed Lady
Montreville foreshadows Lady Catherine de Burgh in *Pride and
Prejudice*, whilst her daughter, who combines snobbery with sexual
jealousy in her attitude to Emmeline, is not unlike Miss Bingley.

A sub-plot centres around the unhappy Lady Adelina, who is
pining away from remorse and in deep obscurity after an extra-
marital liaison has left her pregnant. But it is significant that
Emmeline and her independent friend Mrs Stafford, who is rather
like Mrs Arlbery and Mrs Selwyn in the novels of Burney, befriend
the unhappy Adelina and look after her during and after her
pregnancy. No Burney heroine would have been allowed to mix in
such company, and the normal attitude expressed in the conservative
courtship novel is that no young lady should risk her reputation by
associating with women of doubtful reputation, and even such
women never have illegitimate children. But Charlotte Smith's
heroine constantly expresses active sympathy for women in distress.
During a journey Godolphin, the hero, befriends the wife of an
officer who is in difficulties, but does not introduce her to Emmeline
and Mrs Stafford, who are also on the road. He explains his reason:
'I know not whether I might not be deceived in the character of
Mrs Stornaway; and dared not intrude upon you, lest it should be
found that the object merited not your good offices.' Whereupon

Emmeline immediately answers: 'But she is in distress! . . . She is a stranger! – and shall we hesitate?'[13]

Burney's constant ambivalence about unconventional women makes it doubtful whether she consciously identified with the forceful Mrs Arlbery, but there is no doubt about the identification of Charlotte Smith with Mrs Stafford, since the wayward and unreliable Mr Stafford was a pen portrait of the author's husband. When Lady Adelina is first discovered by the two women Mrs Stafford suspects her to be an unfortunate woman seduced by her own husband, but this does not prevent her from giving assistance. On the contrary. And when Delamere sees Emmeline with Adelina's baby and breaks off the engagement because he thinks Emmeline is the mother, Mrs Stafford tells Emmeline that he has only himself to blame and that she should offer no explanation. And that if he does not come round she is well rid of him. Which, of course, she is, since she never loved him in the first place and has since met Godolphin.

It transpires that Emmeline was legitimate and proud Lord Montreville, having lost his son Delamere, who dies as a result of a duel, is forced to hand over Emmeline's fortune with interest. No doubt these were the 'false expectations' which Wollstonecraft condemned, but Charlotte Smith had scored a good many points *en route* to her conventional ending. If Lord Montreville had not been so intransigent, he would not have lost his beloved son, the chief object of his pride. Delamere himself is the victim of an over-indulgent education. Social convention makes Charlotte Smith hesitate to give Lady Adelina a happy ending: we see her, almost dying of remorse, refuse to marry the man she loves, who is also the father of her child. When she refuses her adoring and penitent lover on the grounds that she is not worthy to be his wife and must be punished, the only authorial justification seems to be that her decision inflicts almost more pain on the man involved. Apart, of course, from the need to avoid outraging conventional morality too much by rewarding such heinous sin with happiness. But before the author ties up all the loose ends in conventional knots she has had her heroine weeping over Adelina's baby son:

> whose birth, so similar to her own, seemed to render it to her a more interesting and affecting object. She lamented the evils to which it might be exposed; tho' of a sex which would prevent it's encountering the same species of sorrow as that which had embittered her own life.[14]

Charlotte Smith is more expressly feminist than Burney, or at least the early Burney. But this statement helps us to understand why, in *Evelina* just as much as in *Emmeline*, to say nothing of countless other women's novels, the authors chose a heroine who stood alone, orphaned, possibly illegitimate, outside the privileged protection of society. It was a way of highlighting the essential vulnerability of all women.

Emmeline ends, as it began, with a touch of the Gothics. Staying with Adelina at Godolphin's home on the Isle of Wight, she is frightened by a nightly apparition (who soon turns out to be Adelina's penitent lover):

> All breathed a certain solemn and melancholy stillness calculated to inspire horror. Emmeline's blood ran cold; yet innocence like her's really fears nothing if free from the prejudices of superstition. She endeavoured to conquer the disagreeable sensations she felt, and to shake off the effects of her dreams . . .[15]

This was to be the keynote of *The Mysteries of Udolpho*. If Mrs Radcliffe was inspired by Charlotte Smith's mildly spooky scenes to elaborate the dark and dreadful, she also elaborated the moral justification for giving her readers the shivers, and that was to conquer irrational fear and unfounded superstition. It is another strand in the developing theme of female fortitude, particularly since women are supposed to be more easily frightened, more nervous of real physical threats, more alarmed by shadows.

Readers who are familiar with *Northanger Abbey* but not with *The Mysteries of Udolpho* will be surprised, on first reading the latter, to find that it is not a wild offspring of the romantic movement but a carefully contrived exposition of eighteenth-century rationalism. The heroine is led through a series of adventures which call on her developing capacity to conquer both her rational and irrational fears. In the early sections of the book she is constantly starting at shadows, the victim of fears without foundation, a child who is superstitiously afraid of the dark. Later she is exposed to a series of situations where it is necessary to distinguish between illusion and reality, where she has to cope with a mixture of real physical danger and a series of optical illusions intended to rouse her superstitious fear, and it is only by conquering her irrational fears that she is able to cope with the very real dangers that beset her.

However, the book itself is something of an illusion. Radcliffe employs distancing devices which have the effect of cushioning her heroine from real harm and reassuring her readers, who can thus shudder with pleasure rather than fear, and it is with these distancing devices that Jane Austen is really arguing, as we shall see, in *Northanger Abbey*. To begin with, Radcliffe sets her story abroad, in a France and Italy of the past, and of such dubious historical accuracy that it might as well be fantasy-land. Radcliffe not only makes no attempt to convince the reader that the events really are taking place in the sixteenth century, but allows so many obvious anachronisms that she is clearly indicating to the reader that she is creating a charade, a costume drama, for the sake of licence. Her heroine is an eighteenth-century girl undergoing imaginary trials and adventures which would not be possible or proper in real life.

Another distancing device is her descriptions of scenery. These are many, and very elaborate, as her heroine travels through Europe, and provided a vicarious Grand Tour for female readers who were forced to stay at home while their more fortunate brothers travelled. But Radcliffe always builds up her pictures of scenery as though she was describing paintings in a frame. She may indeed have been inspired by actual paintings, as her writing suggests, and she certainly did not visit the places she describes in such painterly detail. But the fact that she always wrote as though she was describing paint on canvas, described scenic effects for their artistic qualities, and did not write as though she was depicting real mountains, rocks and air, is significant. Her scenes, however wild and romantic, are always rendered innocuous because they are framed. The reader, like the heroine, is looking at a picture, or is set off against it, she is never actually *in* it. She travels across France and over the Alps, looks at the scenery with awe and feelings of sublime wonder without ever getting bumped, ruffled, worn out or soaked to the skin.

So, in a sense, *Udolpho* is consistent with the attitude to the novel expressed by Dr Johnson and Burney, in teaching the young about the evils of life without actually exposing them to danger. And since the dangers in this novel are of an extreme kind Radcliffe uses distancing devices to show the reader that these dangers are in fact theoretical.[16] Since the didactic message of the book is that one should learn to distinguish illusion from reality, it is appropriate that the book itself should be a transparent illusion.

Novels of the period were constantly warning young women of the dangers of sensibility. Yet how could they ever learn to overcome this female frailty in real-life conditions which did everything to foster this weakness? The fantasy adventures of Emily were one answer to the problem, at least by example. At the beginning of the story, when Emily is still living in peaceful seclusion with her father, unaware of the horrors which lie ahead, her father is already striving to fortify her for the trials of life:

> She had discovered in her early years uncommon delicacy of mind, warm affections, and ready benevolence; but with these was observable a degree of susceptibility too exquisite to admit of lasting peace. As she advanced in youth, this sensibility gave a pensive tone to her spirits, and a softness to her manner, which added grace to beauty, and rendered her a very interesting object to persons of a congenial disposition. But St Aubert had too much good sense to prefer a charm to a virtue; and had penetration enough to see that this charm was too dangerous to its possessor to be allowed the character of a blessing. He endeavoured, therefore, to strengthen her mind; to inure her to habits of self-command; to teach her to reject the first impulse of her feelings; and to look with cool examination upon the disappointments he sometimes threw in her way. While he instructed her to resist first impressions, and to acquire that steady dignity of mind that can alone counterbalance the passions, and bear us, as far as is compatible with our nature, above the reach of circumstances . . .[17]

Throughout the novel Emily is being tested, ever more rigorously, and the little disappointments which St Aubert teaches his daughter to bear are only the first steps on a hard road. Her mother had died when she was young: 'Never had Emily felt the importance of the lessons which had taught her to restrain her sensibility so much as in these moments and never had she practised them with a triumph so complete.'[18] The next great trial she has to bear is the death of her father, made worse by the fact that she is travelling through alien countryside and far from home. St Aubert duly delivers a final lecture on his deathbed:

> Above all . . . do not indulge in the pride of fine feeling, the romantic error of amiable minds. Those who really possess sensibility ought early to be taught that it is a dangerous quality . . . we become the victims of our feelings, unless we can

in some degree command them . . . I would not teach you to become insensible if I could. I would only warn you of the evils of susceptibility, and point out how you may avoid them. Beware, my love, I conjure you, of that self-delusion which has been fatal to the peace of so many persons – beware of priding yourself on the gracefulness of sensibility . . .. Always remember how much more valuable is the strength of sensibility. Do not, however, confound fortitude with apathy . . .[19]

It is significant that Emily copes better with real disasters, when forced to do so, than with illusory terrors. Nightfall always brings fears, together with romantic sensibility. Radcliffe loves describing night scenes, moonlight, shadows stealing over the peaceful landscape, and the delicious melancholy that goes with such scenes. Her heroine, too, loves to lean out over moonlit sills, but her self-indulgent night thoughts are from the beginning disturbed by illusory fears; even while she is still at home, and long before she reaches the castle of Udolpho, she is alarmed at nights by mysterious sights and sounds, which always, in the end, have a rational explanation. Having learnt to master her first fears, she is exposed to bigger night terrors. Her father's death, in particular, and a somewhat unnecessary visit to his grave at midnight, exposes Emily to mysterious night frights which she tries to conquer, telling herself that melancholy has heightened her susceptibility. The author drives home the message to the reader, safely shivering in her boudoir, no doubt with considerable pleasure:

> The solitary life which Emily had led of late, and the melancholy subjects on which she had suffered her thoughts to dwell, had rendered her at times sensible to the 'thick-coming fancies' of a mind greatly enervated. It was lamentable that her excellent understanding should have yielded, even for a moment, to the reveries of superstition, or rather to those starts of imagination which deceive the senses into what can be called nothing less than momentary madness.[20]

However, even while Radcliffe is constantly bowing to the didactic imperative imposed on the female novelist, and her readers, she is perfectly well aware that fictional terror can be highly enjoyable. As Emily first explores the sinister castle she comments that 'terror of this nature, as it occupies and expands the mind, and elevates it to higher expectation, is purely sublime, and leads us, by a kind of fascination, to seek even the object from which we appear to shrink'.[21]

But at a second, non-didactic level this kind of Gothic novel provided a female equivalent of the male picaresque. It was escapist in a very real sense, since it freed both its female readers and its heroine from the narrow restrictions of a lady's highly civilised existence. The heroine of *Udolpho* travels from place to place, in the process taking her readers on a surrogate Grand Tour which covers the most wild and wonderful scenery in Europe. But propriety demands that young ladies should not travel about unchaperoned, exposing themselves to danger, a fact which normally put the picaresque tradition out of the female novelist's reach. But in *Udolpho*, a novel essentially developed from the abduction plot, the problem of female propriety and restriction is overcome by making the heroine act under duress, and not of her own volition. She leaves home, initially, not to seek adventure or fortune as a young man might do, but under the chaperonage of her father, who is forced to travel to sort out his financial affairs. Her father dies on the journey, leaving her unprotected. She then comes under the chaperonage of her aunt, who lives in Italy, necessitating a further journey (and in eighteenth-century fiction Italy was described as a land of bandits, vendettas, and passionate men). Her aunt has married the evil Montoni, master of the remote castle Udolpho, to which he transports his unsuspecting wife and her niece. The aunt dies in captivity and Emily is under a double duress from Montoni, to give up her inheritance and agree to a forced marriage for the same end. At the same time Emily is under constant sexual threat, since the corridors and secret passages are full of lustful men trying to get at her, and Montoni declines to protect her. She is put in a room which has a door to a secret passage, and this door cannot be locked from the inside. Under such circumstances both feminist fortitude and conventional propriety make it imperative for Emily to make her escape from the castle and travel back to France as best she can, unchaperoned and alone. And although Emily meets her future husband very early on in the narrative the author keeps him out of the way for the main body of the story so that Emily can be seen to act on her own. She finally returns to France to marry him, with estate and honour intact.

Udolpho also flirts with sexual danger. In the conventional courtship novel of the period sexual passion was quite excluded, unless there was a sub-plot of abduction. And the plot of abduction tended to be ugly, brutish and short, with a long aftermath of misery and remorse. But Emily, trapped in an architectural maze of stairways and corridors, underground passages and hidden doorways, is constantly at risk from men who remain in the shadows, anonymous and unknown. Just as the surreal building is full of unknown perils, illusory and real, so its inhabitants are made up of friends and enemies, and Emily must learn to tell them apart. It is the subconscious world not just of sexual danger, but of desirable danger. Its night landscape will be familiar to any woman who remembers early dreams of pursuit which somehow never ended in capture. But the distancing devices already referred to serve to reassure the reader: the whole thing is a fantasy, Emily will remain untouched by rapacious male lust just as she remains untouched by wind and weather during her travels, and the sexual innuendo remains largely implicit. This is the true 'terror' which 'leads us, by a kind of fascination, to seek even the object from which we appear to shrink'. Such fascinated terror, where subconscious desire leads the mind to replay constant variants of the same theme of pursuit, is a clear result of repression. In a sense the Gothic novel, while preaching the same virtues, also provided a safety valve – at least in fantasy – for the sexual repression actively promoted by women's novels which constantly hammered home the necessity for prudence and self-control in the passional sphere.

It was this psychic, subconscious level that appealed to other and later women writers, and made them borrow Gothic elements from Mrs Radcliffe. (I should perhaps point out here that male exponents of the Gothic novel had quite different aims and intentions.) Montoni himself is a mixture of attraction and repulsion, modelled on Milton's Satan, who was to surface again and again in women's fiction, wilful, Byronic, ruthless, but with a fatal attraction. In *Udolpho* only Emily's aunt falls for him, while the heroine remains impervious to his sexual power. In later novels, particularly those of the Brontës, such black heroes would play a far more central role.

Through the Gothic novel the theme of imprisonment took on a new, far less realistic dimension. Familiar through reading, the imagery was readily to hand for women who were trying to express, not conventional wisdom, but the bitter frustration of women's lives.

When Mary Wollstonecraft died in 1797 she left behind an unfinished novel called *Maria* or *The Wrongs of Woman*, which was published posthumously. Wollstonecraft was essentially a polemicist rather than a novelist. The world of the imagination did not come naturally to her, but on this occasion, by adopting a Gothic framework, she found a power and fluency which had so far been markedly absent from her fiction.

Wollstonecraft's heroine is locked up in a dark and gloomy house, with a female wardress, Jemima, who gradually befriends the heroine and is herself the victim of social deprivation. There is a curious ambiguity about the exact nature of the house in which Maria is imprisoned on the orders of her husband. It seems to be a lunatic asylum, but at least some of the people incarcerated in it are clearly quite sane. It is essentially a private prison under cover of being an asylum, for people who are victims of those more powerful than themselves. At the same time it is a dark and dreadful place of the mind, and it is this ambiguity about the nature of this strange mansion, curiously devoid of officials, doctors or warders, apart from Jemima, which gives the setting unusual power and resonance. Women are the victims of men, but as a result they have also become the prisoners of their own minds. The house, such a central image in women's novels, takes on a new dimension. In the clear light of the courtship novel it represents security and status. The house of the bridegroom, into which the heroine will move after marriage, is always of prime importance. For Austen's Elizabeth marrying Darcy means living at Pemberley, and Emma shows her appreciation of Mr Knightley's residence long before she becomes aware of her feelings for its owner. Mansfield Park represents a whole way of life and a distinct set of values. But in the Gothic novel the house changes from being a symbol of male privilege and protection conferred on the fortunate female of his choice, to an image of male power in its sinister aspect, threatening and oppressive. Charming vistas, gardens, drawing rooms and library are replaced by heavy doors which clang shut, iron bars, chains, battlements and dungeons. For the mind of woman the marital home is a prison, rank with the smell of decay and death, which threatens to drive her insane.

In *Udolpho* Emily, in spite of all the real and illusory horrors which beset her, overcomes her difficulties and remains sane and controlled; of course, since the whole purpose of the novel, the didactic purpose at least, is to show the necessity of rational self-control. All the weird apparitions she sees have a rational explanation by the last chapter, however contrived. Apart from the real dangers represented by Montoni and his followers, Udolpho is a contrived chamber of horrors full of wax images and mechanical contraptions and, having come out into the daylight, we are told how everything worked. But Wollstonecraft's prison house has become the world of the repressed subconscious, the imprisoned soul:

> Often at midnight was she waked by the dismal shrieks of demoniac rage, or of excruciating despair, uttered in such wild tones of indescribable anguish as proved the total absence of reason, and roused phantoms of horror in her mind . . . . It was the uproar of the passions which she was compelled to observe.[22]

Charlotte Brontë's Jane Eyre, on coming to Thornfield Hall, also heard shrieks of demoniac rage in the night. In *Jane Eyre* she showed that the house of man had two distinct faces. The home which Mr Rochester offers Jane seems, on the surface and during daylight hours, to be all that a woman could desire, and Jane, like so many heroines, is a penniless orphan, so that the house seems to offer love and luxury beyond her wildest hopes. But at night, in the darkness of the soul, the house becomes a prison. Shrieks of despair and rage are heard. The woman who becomes Mrs Rochester will go mad, and turn on her warder in a frenzy of despair. It is only through the destruction of the house that a resolution is arrived at.

If, for the female imagination, the Gothic mode provided an escape from the narrowness of convention, a dark underworld which necessarily counterbalanced the insistent clarity of common day, it ultimately found its way back to a new mainstream synthesis of dark and light, objective reality and subjective vision.

6. The Supremacy of Sense

WHILST the lives of upper-class young women, the main readers of women's fiction, were so restricted, any attempt to widen the horizon of heroines was fraught with difficulty. Jane Austen understood that in the interests of credibility, to say nothing of artistry, a heroine's adventures should be minimal. With her lifelong instinct for parody, an essential corner-stone to her art, she wrote a 'Plan of a novel according to hints from various quarters'[1] which is worth quoting almost in full because it contains all the elements of the female fortitude novel, and is particularly close to Mary Brunton's *Self-Control*, which Austen read without much enthusiasm:

> Heroine to be the daughter of a clergyman, who after living much in the world had retired from it, and settled on a curacy with a very small fortune of his own. The most excellent man that can be imagined, perfect in character, temper, and manner, without the smallest drawback or peculiarity to prevent his being the most delightful companion to his daughter from one year's end to the other. Heroine faultless in character, beautiful in person, and possessing every possible accomplishment. Book to open with father and daughter conversing in long speeches, elegant language, and a tone of high serious sentiment. The father induced, at his daughter's earnest request, to relate to her the past events of his life. Narrative to reach through the greater part of the first volume; as besides all the circumstances of his attachment to her mother, and their marriage, it will comprehend his going to sea as chaplain to a distinguished naval character about the court; and his going afterwards to court himself, which involved him in many interesting situations, concluding with his opinion of the benefit of tithes being done away with . . . . From this outset the story will proceed, and contain a striking variety of adventures. Father an exemplary parish priest, and devoted to literature; but heroine and father never above a fortnight in one place: he being driven from his curacy by the vile arts of some totally unprincipled and heartless young man, desperately in love with the heroine, and pursuing her

with unrelenting passion. No sooner settled in one country in Europe, than they are compelled to quit it, and retire to another, always making new acquaintance, and always obliged to leave them. This will of course exhibit a wide variety of character. The scene will be for ever shifting from one set of people to another, but there will be no mixture, all the good will be unexceptionable in every respect. There will be no foibles or weaknesses but with the wicked, who will be completely depraved and infamous, hardly a resemblance of humanity left in them. Early in her career, the heroine will meet with the hero: all perfection, of course, and only prevented from paying his addresses to her by some excess of refinement. Wherever she goes, somebody falls in love with her, and she receives repeated offers of marriage, which she refers wholly to her father, exceedingly angry that *he* should not be the first applied to. Often carried away by the anti-hero, but rescued either by her father or the hero. Often reduced to support herself and her father by her talents, and work for her bread; continually cheated, and defrauded of her hire; worn down to a skeleton, and now and then starved to death. At last, hunted out of civilised society, denied the poor shelter of the humblest cottage, they are compelled to retreat into Kamtschatka, where the poor father quite worn down, finding his end approaching, throws himself on the ground, and after four or five hours of tender advice and parental admonition to his miserable child, expires in a fine burst of literary enthusiasm, intermingled with invectives against the holders of tithes. Heroine inconsolable for some time, but afterwards crawls back towards her former country, having at least twenty narrow escapes of falling into the hands of anti-hero; and at last, in the very nick of time, turning a corner, to avoid him, runs into the arms of the hero himself, who, having just shaken off the scruples which fettered him before, was at the very moment setting off in pursuit of her. The tenderest and completest *éclaircissement* takes place, and they are happily united. Throughout the whole work heroine to be in the most elegant society, and living in high style.

This is not only a fairly accurate synthesis of many of the forgotten novels of the period, and some of those which are not wholly forgotten, like *Udolpho*, but it also highlights some of the characteristics of their plots which Austen reacted against in her own work. The meandering implausibility of the female picaresque, the sentimental relationship between father and daughter, for which her Mr Woodhouse was to provide such a wonderful corrective, the tendency for characters to be either black or white, with 'no foibles or weaknesses but with the wicked', whilst hero and heroine have no faults at all; and the plethora of passionate suitors who seemed to surround such a heroine. Life, Austen is saying in this parody, is not like that.

But to say that Jane Austen was a realist would also be false. Fathers do die, young women do fall upon hard times and are exploited in trying to earn a living, and such events are conspicuously absent from Austen's own novels. With her strong sense of the absurd, her avid appetite for fiction from an early age, Austen was from the start weighing up the possibilities of fiction as much as the possibilities of life. Sensing the contradictions involved in a women's fiction which, while preaching prudence and propriety, was struggling to widen imaginative and affective horizons, she came down firmly on the side of prudence and propriety, aligned herself, like most of her female contemporaries, on the side of English sense as opposed to foreign sensibility, but at the same time made her texts apparently coherent and consistent by excluding such elements as death or sexual passion.

Up to a point this must have been a self-protective mechanism. In *Pride and Prejudice* the adjective 'sensible' is used with obsessive frequency. She was highly pleased when an acquaintance praised *Mansfield Park* as the most 'sensible' novel he had ever read,[2] which seems faint praise to us. Her letters, those that survive, show a tendency to brittle sarcasm: 'Mrs Hall, of Sherborne, was brought to bed yesterday of a dead child, some weeks before she expected, owing to a fright. I suppose she happened unawares to look at her husband.'[3] An unkind remark which, if made by one of her own heroines, say Emma, would have earned her a severe rebuke from Mr Knightley. But Austen the novelist is allowed a licence not permitted to her own female characters. When her niece Anna got married she wrote: 'Her Letters have been very sensible and satisfactory, with no *parade* of happiness, which I liked them the better for. – I have often known young married women write in a way I did not like in that respect.'[4] This avoidance of sentiment, of a '*parade* of happiness', also characterises her fiction. No doubt there is irony in the letter, but also a self-protective shield of sense from possible jealousy. What is more ironic, after all, than the lifelong spinster writing of matrimony?

In Austen there is none of the surface tension we find in Burney between natural feelings and the demands of society, so that her narrative seems to pull in two directions at once; she did not, like Edgeworth, switch from a highly critical view of the world (*Castle Rackrent*) to a highly conformist one (*Belinda*) because of outside pressure. No, from the start Austen's work shows a logical consistency which has beguiled and deceived generations of admiring male readers, who have so often failed to perceive the ambiguity which underlies so much of her work.

At the age of fourteen Jane Austen had already written her hilarious burlesque, *Love and Freindship*, which is totally consistent with her later work. Already she is familiar with contemporary female fiction, and has decided on its more obvious absurdities. She makes fun of the perfect heroine: 'the graces of my Person were the least of my Perfections. Of every accomplishment accustomary to my sex, I was Mistress.' She disapproves of sensibility and unlike her contemporaries, gives some logic to her disapproval by associating it with selfishness, as she would later in *Sense and Sensibility*: 'A sensibility too tremblingly alive to every affliction of my Freinds, my Acquaintance and particularly to every affliction of my own, was my only fault, if a fault it could be called.' She mocks the idea of love at first sight, the 'First Impressions' the novelist of sense so often warned against: Laura no sooner sees the stranger who has knocked at the door 'than I felt that on him the happiness or Misery of my future Life must depend'. The idea of marrying against parental wishes is shown as rebellion for its own sake: 'Lady Dorothea is lovely and Engaging; I prefer no woman to her; but know Sir, that I scorn to marry her in compliance with your wishes. No! Never shall it be said that I obliged my Father.' On hearing this protest the father asks where his son has picked up such 'unmeaning Gibberish' and adds ruefully: 'You have been studying Novels I suspect.' Showing that Austen was already aware of the ambiguity involved in writing fiction, and the need to project the correct values.

And already at the age of fourteen Austen understood that sensibility was not only silly and selfish, but impracticable, when filial duty was combined with filial dependence. In her novels we always know exactly what everybody is worth in terms of money; in *Love and Freindship* Sophia and Augustus, having married against their parents' wishes, lived on money 'purloined from his Unworthy father's Escritoire'. They soon get into debt and their idyll ends when Augustus is duly arrested. Edward, also defying his father on the question of matrimony, is reminded by his sister that he may need paternal support in the form of 'Victuals and Drink', which elicits the romantic response: 'Can you not conceive the Luxury of living in every Distress that Poverty can inflict, with the object of your tenderest Affection?' Hearing which, his sensible sister snaps: 'You are too ridiculous to argue with'.

Most of her contemporaries understood the impracticality of disobeying parental wishes and the imprudence of young women following the instinct of their own feelings, but they tended to find the moral justification for such behaviour by emphasising female duty and submission. Austen gave her conservative stance of 'sense' a more consistent and enduring validity by relating sense and duty to the cohesion of the community, to being a good neighbour as well as a good daughter. Again sense is being related to unselfishness. This connection is already there in *Love and Freindship*, where sensibility is equated with selfishness:

> Our time was most delightfully spent, in mutual Protestations of Freindship, and in vows of unalterable Love, in which we were secure from being interrupted, by intruding and disagreeable Visitors, as Augustus & Sophia had on their first Entrance into the Neighbourhood, taken due care to inform the surrounding Families, that as their Happiness centered wholly in themselves, they wished for no other society.

And when the two husbands are imprisoned for debt Sophia refuses to visit her husband in Newgate because the sight would 'overpower' her sensibility, much as Edgeworth's Lady Olivia refuses to visit Leonora's sick and highly infectious husband in *Leonora* on the same grounds. Sensibility is not only selfish, it is a skin-deep affectation.

Male admirers of Jane Austen, disturbed by the undertones of her work, and to reassure themselves and their students of her essential female amiability, are apt to quote her advice to her niece, never to marry without affection, as though this somehow proved that she was a true woman at heart. However she also wrote to her wavering niece: 'There *are* such beings in the World perhaps, one in a Thousand, as the Creature You and I should think Perfection . . . but such a person may not come your way, or if he does, he may not be the eldest son of a Man of Fortune, the Brother of your particular friend, & belonging to your own County'[5], all important attributes for her heroes. And then she actually wrote: 'Anything is to be preferred or endured rather than marrying without Affection' and goes on, having made the proposed marriage sound like a crucifixion: 'I have no doubt of his suffering a good deal for a time . . . but it is no creed of mine, as you must be well aware, that such sort of Disappointments kill anybody.' The ambiguity of her fiction, lying just below the surface certainties, became vacillating uncertainty when applied to a problem of real life, where women had such few choices. Her own distrust of marriage, so obvious in the letters, even if it is partly attributable to sour grapes (though not when she writes to Fanny Knight), is echoed by Fanny Burney who, when she married in middle age, admitted to a friend: 'I had never made any vow against Marriage, but I had LONG - LONG been firmly persuaded it was – *for ME* – a state of too much hazard, & too little promise, to draw me from my individual plans & purposes.'[6]

Already in *Love and Freindship* we see a tendency to discount the value of sexual passion between man and woman, to see it as a destructive force in opposition to the social ties of family. This in itself is fairly conventional at a time when affection rather than sexual passion was seen as the true basis of marriage, and when young women were being advised, through conservative fiction, to obey their parents and let judgement and reason rather than passion govern their marriage choice. But in her juvenilia we see Austen debunking a good deal more than romantic elopements. Freindship between women, for instance. In *Love and Freindship*, she writes, with obvious irony: 'She was all Sensibility and Feeling. We flew into each other arms & after having exchanged vows of mutual Freindship for the rest of our Lives, instantly unfolded to each other the most inward Secrets of our Hearts.' Two years later, in *Lesley Castle*, young Jane Austen uses the epistolary form not only to show women being self-congratulatory and sentimental, but thoroughly bitchy into the bargain. The women correspond in tones of surface affection which hides a vicious competitiveness. Miss Margaret Lesley finds her own beauty a burden, and writes in a tone of purring hypocrisy to her best friend: 'How often have I wished that I possessed as little personal Beauty as you do.' She refers in derogatory terms to a young man who is 'a little singular in his Taste – he is in love with Matilda'. And of her new stepmother: 'I do not think her so pretty as you seem to consider her.' Meanwhile the stepmother is writing to the same confidante, unaware of the other correspondence, that her stepdaughters are plain, over-grown girls.

This is all very amusing, of course, and provides a refreshing corrective to *Sir Charles Grandison*, for example, where women not only write the most flattering letters to each other but even compete with each other in giving up the man they love when they think someone else has a more worthy claim. Life, says young Jane, is not like that, and women are ready to scratch each other's eyes out, while pretending affection. The mature Jane Austen would moderate this early vision of life as a jungle involving a sometimes vicious struggle for survival considerably before she thought herself ready to venture into print. This uncomfortable vision still underlies her early *Northanger Abbey*, which was sold to a publisher but for some reason did not see the light of day until after her death fifteen years later.

At a superficial reading *Northanger Abbey* seems to be making fun of the Gothic novel. It is a continuation of her juvenilia in that, though not quite parody or burlesque, her initial inspiration is still from other literature, which she rejects and finds absurd. Again Austen is saying 'Life is not like that', but as in her juvenilia she does not stop there, but gives an alternative vision of what life *is* like, and that is just as unpleasant, and in some ways not dissimilar. At a superficial level Jane Austen appears to be setting common sense against fanciful illusion, in the tradition of her time. But at another level she is criticising Radcliffe for the distancing devices discussed in the previous chapter, the fancy-dress setting in a foreign country of an unlikely sixteenth century, which has the effect of giving the reader a sense of reassurance and security. A false sense of security, according to the Austen of this early period.

Conservative women writers of this period tended to praise England and the English way of life. English sense was contrasted with French sensibility or anarchic German romanticism, and English domestic arrangements were considered superior to anything on the continent, particularly the education of young women as companionate wives. Edgeworth in particular, having visited France, loved to compare the quiet domestic bliss of a well-regulated English household with the flirtation, coquetry and public display practised in French society after marriage. Austen, too, though usually less explicit on the subject, expresses pro-English attitudes. Mr Knightley is not only a gentleman, he is very much an English country gentleman, and his Englishness is part of his particular virtue. By the time she wrote *Mansfield Park*, her most ambitious novel and a conscious step forward after three novels written in a much more playful way, with other literature very much in mind, she was consciously trying to schematise both her conservatism and her sense of England, and one was part of the other. By the time she wrote *Emma* her pro-English attitudes had become much more natural, and one has a sense of deep underlying affection.

But the young Jane Austen had a much sharper, more cynical eye, as her juvenilia shows, and it had not faded by the time she wrote *Northanger Abbey*. As a result, since she was by now writing for possible publication, it is her most sharply ambiguous book. At first glance Catherine Morland, partly through youth and inexperience, has allowed her imagination to run away with her; since Mrs Radcliffe is responsible for her over-vivid fears and fancies the novel also fits into the contemporary mode of showing the ill-effects of reading the wrong kinds of novels. She is deficient, in short, in sense, and when her male mentor Henry Tilney reminds her that she is in England his rebuke not only vindicates common sense but the status quo, and a whole way of life:

> Remember the country and the age in which we live. Remember that we are English, that we are Christians. Consult your own understanding, your own sense of the probable, your own observation of what is passing around you – Does your education prepare us for such atrocities? Do our laws connive at them? Could they be perpetrated without being known, in a country like this, where social and literary intercourse is on such a footing . . . . Dearest Miss Morland, what ideas have you been admitting?[7]

It is a speech that has often been quoted as encapsulating the author's own attitude, the very core of the book. In a way it is, but appearances are deceptive. Readers have been lulled into a false sense of security by the very certainties which Henry Tilney voices.

When Henry makes this speech Catherine has been exploring his father's house in secret, convinced from her reading of Gothic novels that General Tilney had been cruel to his wife, and in some way responsible for her death. Caught out in this dire suspicion and rebuked by Henry, she reaches the nadir of humiliation:

The visions of romance were over. Catherine was completely awakened . . ... Most grievously was she humbled. Most bitterly did she cry. It was not only with herself that she was sunk – but with Henry. Her folly, which now seemed even criminal, was all exposed to him, and he must despise her for ever. The liberty which her imagination had dared to take with the character of his father, could he ever forgive it? The absurdity of her curiosity and her fears, could they ever be forgotten? She hated herself more than she could express.[8]

There is both irony and ambiguity in this opening of a new chapter, which is also the opening of a new phase in the novel. The 'visions of romance' are twofold, those inspired by Mrs Radcliffe, and those inspired by Henry himself. Thoroughly humiliated by the male assurance of his common sense, rebuked for her irrational fears about the nature of the world in which she lives, she feels she must have forfeited any claim to his affection. But when she does see him again 'the only difference in his behaviour to her, was that he paid her rather more attention than usual. Catherine had never wanted comfort more, and he looked as if he was aware of it.' Having established his male dominance and authority by proving her to be a foolish little woman, Henry is ready to be kind. This has little to do with visions of romance, but Austen makes it clear in the novel that for Henry Tilney Catherine's very stupidity, the fact that he can impose his own ideas on her, is the chief attraction.

The irony lies in the fact that other romantic visions are about to be shattered. England, this civilised Christian country, can treat a woman in a barbarous fashion with impunity. The dreadful assessment of General Tilney's character which the imaginative Catherine had dared to conjure up proves to be accurate when he turns her out of the house because she is not an heiress, as he had been led to imagine. Montoni imprisons Emily to try and force her into a marriage to get hold of her fortune; General Tilney, having lured her into his Abbey to marry her off to his son, also for money, summarily kicks her out without ceremony or chaperone when he finds she is not rich. Emily, having escaped from Udolpho, has to travel home as best she can through Italy to her native France, whilst Catherine makes (for her) a no less momentous journey home, upset and tearful, in a humble post-chaise. She soon recovers, but General Tilney is not what he seems:

Without suffering any romantic alarm, in the consideration of their daughter's long and lonely journey, Mr and Mrs Morland could not but feel that it might have been productive of much unpleasantness to her; that it was what they could never have voluntarily suffered; and that, in forcing her on such a measure, General Tilney had acted neither honourably nor feelingly – neither as a gentleman nor as a parent.[9]

Maria Edgeworth thought General Tilney's behaviour ridiculous and improbable, but *Northanger Abbey* was not published until 1818, two decades after it was written. Yet at the close of the eighteenth century the young Maria was writing a first novel which displayed a similar view of human nature, particularly with regard to men's treatment of women. In *Castle Rackrent* the loyal Irish steward Thady innocently recounts a family saga of drink, dissipation and debt in the household he serves with such devotion. We are told that one Rackrent imprisoned his wife for seven years because she refused to give up her jewels:

> Her diamond cross, was, they say, at the bottom of it all; and it was a shame for her, being his wife, not to show more duty, and to have given it up when he condescended to ask so often for such a bit of a trifle in his distresses, especially when he all along made it no secret he married for money.

At this point in the saga Edgeworth, perhaps trying to counter the suspicion that she had been reading too many Gothic novels and was a victim of fanciful imaginings, added a footnote explaining that this part of her narrative was based on the true story of 'the celebrated Lady Cathcart's conjugal imprisonment', Lady Cathcart being locked up for several years because she would not part from her diamonds. Thady regards his master's behaviour as normal and understandable, but so, it seems, did the historic originals:

> Her Ladyship was locked up in her own house for many years; during which period her husband was visited by the neighbouring gentry, and it was his regular custom at dinner to send his compliments to Lady Cathcart, informing her that the company had the honor to drink to her ladyship's health, and begging to know whether there was any thing at table that she would like to eat?

None of the neighbouring gentry saw fit to help the poor woman, who was not released until the death of her husband. By that time she had been incarcerated for over twenty years and 'her understanding seemed stupified'. In Edgeworth's novel the wife who is so abused for her money is Jewish, which helps to emphasise the fact that she is regarded by Thady as an outsider, as any bride would be in that situation, and underlines Thady's prejudices:

> The bride might well be a great fortune – she was *Jewish* by all accounts, who are famous for their great riches. I had never seen any of that tribe or nation before, and could only gather that she spoke a strange kind of English of her own, that she could not abide pork or sausages, and went neither to church nor mass. – Mercy upon his honor's poor soul, thought I, what will become of him, and his, and all of us, with this heretic Blackamore at the head of the Castle Rackrent estate. I never slept a wink all night for thinking of it, but before the servants I put my pipe in my mouth and kept my mind to myself; for I had a great regard for the family, and after this when strange gentlemen's servants came to the house, and would begin to talk about the bride, I took care to put the best foot foremost, and passed her for a Nabob, in the kitchen . . ..

Immediately after the honeymoon Sir Kit begins to torment his Jewish bride by ordering pork for the dinner table. Thady's 'great regard for the family', by which he means the male descendants of the line, is such that he always sides with Sir Kit when he victimises his wife. When she finally regains her liberty after his death in a duel Thady relates that she left Ireland, having taken an 'unaccountable prejudice against the country'. His loyalty is just as unquestioning on other matters. Sir Condy having stood for Parliament, Thady feels that his master 'was very ill used by the government about a place that was promised him and never given, after his supporting them against his conscience very honorably'.

The constant irony in this novel is delicious, and the narrative technique superb. Although set in the past, and in Ireland, it shows that the young Maria Edgeworth had absolutely no illusions about the corrupt and immoral nature of the society which men controlled. While the young Jane Austen took her inspiration from literature, Edgeworth took it from life. *Castle Rackrent* has no literary antecedents, in the narrator she took what her ear heard on arriving in Ireland, and the range of her cynical wisdom is, in this book, far wider than Austen's. Money and politics are easy targets for her, and she hits home with assurance.

The minds of both the youthful Austen and the youthful Edgeworth had an extraordinary incisive quality which, had they been born men, would have been allowed to flourish and develop, but which in a woman had to be subdued or controlled. Austen, who was much more consciously writing in a female literary tradition, who began with parody and was able to hide behind literary mimicry, therefore shows a more consistent literary development. Edgeworth, on the other hand, whose *Castle Rackrent* is a highly original work totally outside any kind of female literary tradition, had to force herself into it in order to find an acceptable social niche. Immediately after *Castle Rackrent*, under the tutelage of her father, she did what women writers were expected to do, and produced a didactic, conservative courtship novel, *Belinda*.

At this stage, having been newly taken in hand by her father, one is conscious of two Maria Edgeworths ill at ease with each other: the dutiful pupil of Richard Lovell Edgeworth, preaching rationalism and the importance of education, and the high-spirited young author of *Castle Rackrent* having fun. The dutiful daughter produced a boring heroine, Belinda, who goes through all the conventional stages of the courtship novel, learning the wisdom of rational judgement in the choice of a mate. The other Maria created Lady Delacour, a sprightly cynic and lady of fashion who has clearly failed to choose the right husband, who mocks her husband instead of honouring him, is that dreadful female aberration, a 'wit', does all the things a lady should not do and nevertheless runs away with the book. Without Lady Delacour *Belinda* would be a tedious tract; because of her the book has a sparkle reminiscent of the best Restoration comedy, and we tolerate the conventional morality. Apparently contemporary readers felt much the same: from Edgeworth's letters it becomes clear that when people praised the novel to her face it was about Lady Delacour that they enthused.

Lady Delacour is not only an entertaining character, she is also rather touching, which is perhaps the real secret of her success, and shows Edgeworth's originality in creating her. Capricious, cynical, married to a man who is her intellectual inferior, Lady Delacour plays at life and breaks most of the rules of conduct imposed on

women, not because she is vicious or depraved, not because she has
been misled by foreign literature (she is too intelligent for that), but
because she is unhappy. The very lifelike bickering that goes on in the
Delacour household while Belinda is staying there provides a sharp
contrast to her later stay with the Percivals, a household which is a
model of peaceful domestic bliss, based on a marriage which is 'a
union of interests, occupations, taste and affection'. Lady Delacour
did not follow the rational precepts which lead to such a union. 'With
me,' she confesses, 'esteem ever followed affection, instead of
affection following esteem. – Wo be to all, who in morals
preposterously put the cart before the horse!'[10]

Mr Percival, who had once been in love with Lady Delacour,
before her marriage, did not put the cart before the horse. As Lady
Delacour amusingly explains: ' . . . he was in love with me, but not
with my faults; now I, wisely considering, that my faults were the
greatest part of me, insisted upon his being in love with my
faults. – He wouldn't, or couldn't.'[11] Whereupon, instead of
correcting her faults, as Austen's Emma would try to do, she married
Delacour out of pique. In Lady Anne, however, Percival found the
ideal mate for a companionate marriage:

> Lady Anne Percival had, without any pedantry or ostentation,
> much accurate knowledge, and a taste for literature which made
> her the chosen companion of her husband's understanding, as well
> as of his heart. He was not obliged to reserve his conversation for
> friends of his own sex, nor was he forced to seclude himself in the
> pursuit of any branch of knowledge; the partner of his warmest
> affections was also the partner of his most serious occupations
> . . . .[12]

It is with the Percivals that Belinda discusses the pitfalls that await a
young woman in choosing a husband, and such familiar topics as the
importance of esteem and the need to avoid being taken in by first
impressions. A misguided feminist, Mrs Freke, involves Lady
Delacour in more folly, and elicits appropriate male conventional
wisdom from Mr Percival: ' . . . women who love to set the world at
defiance in trifles, seldom respect it's opinion in matters of
consequence . . .. They defy the world – the world in turn
excommunicates them – the female outlaw becomes desperate, and
make it the business and pride of their lives to disturb the peace of

their sober neighbours.'[13] Mrs Freke, much more of an absurd
caricature than the 'masculine' women of Fanny Burney, had
persuaded Lady Delacour to fight a duel, and spends her life
beguiling women into 'all kinds of mischief and absurdity'. Once
again one feels that Edgeworth has not really internalised the social
lessons of correct female conduct. Mrs Freke, capering about in male
clothes and fighting duels, is too absurd. But Edgeworth is clearly
trying hard to conform to the dictates of her father. Had he, one
wonders, told her that it was freakish for a young woman to assume
the voice of such a male narrator as Thady? Certainly he was never
heard again. After *Castle Rackrent* Edgeworth's authorial voice is
always that of a lady narrator. Later in her career she became more
relaxed in her writing, but she continued to profess the conventional
female virtues; and although quaint Irish characters reappeared they
were kept firmly in their place.

With *Belinda* Edgeworth is trying to find herself a suitable niche
within the approved tradition of female didacticism, the conservative
courtship novel dedicated to the concept of sense and self-control as
opposed to romanticism and sensibility. The book is signposted with
appropriate literary references, as such books so often are.
Rousseau's supposed ideas are ridiculed in a sub-plot in which a
young woman is brought up as a child of nature, renamed Virginia
after *Paul et Virginie*, and raised in romantic seclusion with
unsatisfactory results: the hero finds her ignorant and indolent, and
by no means a suitable bride. More significantly, the suitor
eventually rejected by Belinda is Mr Vincent, and Mr Percival says
of him:

> Mr Vincent is a lover and a hero. You know it is a ruled case, in all
> romances, that, when a lover and his mistress go out riding
> together, some adventure must befal them. The horse must run
> away with the lady, and the gentleman must catch her in his arms
> just as her neck is about to be broken.[14]

This reminds us of the way Marianne meets the unsuitable
Willoughby in *Sense and Sensibility*, but *Belinda* was published ten years
before Austen's novel. However, Mrs West's *A Gossip's Story* had
been published four years before *Belinda*, and also contained a similar
incident. Mrs West's novel was published in 1797, and according to

Cassandra Austen her sister began work on the first draft of *Sense and Sensibility*, at that stage in epistolary form and entitled *Elinor and Marianne*, in November of that year.

The similarity of plot and theme between *A Gossip's Story* and *Sense and Sensibility*, eventually published in 1811, go beyond the possibility of coincidence, though Jane Austen's novel is incomparably superior in terms of narrative skill. At first sight it seems odd that an artist like Austen should bother to take anything from a third-rate novelist, but one must re-emphasise that for the young Jane Austen, as her juvenilia shows, the starting point was other literature: parody, burlesque, mimicry. As far as we know she was working on all three of her first novels, *Sense and Sensibility, Pride and Prejudice* and *Northanger Abbey*, in a tentative way, at one and the same time, over a period of years, to amuse herself and her family, and all three books are at least partly inspired by, or provoked by, other books, and have strong literary roots.

In *Northanger Abbey* Austen was reacting against the fanciful *Mysteries of Udolpho* with its Italian castle of horrors and providing an alternative, English horror story rooted in contemporary reality, as the name 'North–anger' suggests. Mrs West's novel, on the other hand, promotes the philosophy of sense with which Austen chose to align herself, and her story provided a suitable starting point, though not much more, for a story designed to exemplify the advantages of prudence and good sense and the dangers of romantic sensibility.

Like *Sense and Sensibility*, Mrs West's story concerns two sisters of contrasting temperament. The elder, Louisa, brought up under her widowed father's tuition, with features 'more agreeable than beautiful' has the disposition 'to improve both in moral and mental excellence'; the younger sister who, like Austen's younger sister is called Marianne, has been brought up by her maternal grandmother with 'all the fond indulgence of doating love', and is the beauty:

> . . . her blue eyes swam in sensibility, and the beautiful transparency of her complexion seemed designed to convey to the admiring beholder every varying sentiment of her mind. Her looks expressed what indeed she was, tremblingly alive to all the softer passions. Though the gentle timidity of her temper had preserved her from the usual effects of early indulgence, it rendered her peculiarly unfit to encounter even those common calamities humanity must endure.[15]

Mrs West is inclined to regard the sorrows of 'the softer passions' as not only the result of sensibility, but as self-induced and therefore largely imaginary. In her dedication, where she claims to be illustrating the 'Advantages of CONSISTENCY, FORTITUDE,and the DOMESTICK VIRTUES' as opposed to 'CAPRICE, AFFECTED SENSIBILITY, and an IDLE CENSORIOUS HUMOUR' she writes that she will be 'happy, if while she is instructing her sex how to avoid yielding to imaginary sorrows, she can, for a moment, banish from her dejected heart, the pressure of *real* calamity'. Needless to say Marianne is an avid reader of romances and 'had transplanted into her gentle bosom all the soft feelings and highly refined sensibilities of the respective heroines'.[16] Something that Austen, having championed the novel in *Northanger Abbey*, declines to say overtly about her Marianne. The faults of Marianne Dashwood, like those of Catherine Morland, are attributable to youth and inexperience rather than books or a faulty education.

Mrs West's Marianne is courted by a Mr Pelham, with the support of her father, who has made inquiries about him and discovered him to have all the virtues that Austen afterwards required of her richer suitors, Darcy, Colonel Brandon and Mr Knightley: 'I am told he is a kind master, an indulgent landlord, an obliging neighbour, and a steady active friend.' But Marianne does not find him sufficiently romantic as a suitor, whereupon her father warns her that romantic love does not last and that 'Mr Pelham's character as a man, is of much greater consequence to your future peace, than his behaviour as a lover.'[17]

Mrs West's Marianne, like Austen's, meets the man she does find romantic when Mr Clermont, like Willoughby, rescues her from physical danger, on this occasion from a runaway horse, just the kind of incident referred to in *Belinda* as 'romantic' in a derogatory sense. Austen subdues the incident considerably by making her heroine simply fall and sprain her ankle. Like Willoughby, Clermont visits her the following day, and the two find an immediate similarity of tastes:

Never was such a wonderful coincidence of opinion! Both were passionate admirers of the country; both loved moonlight walks, and the noise of distant waterfalls; both were enchanted by the sound of the sweet-toned harp, and the almost equally soft cadence of the pastoral and elegiack muse; in short, whatever was passionate, elegant, and sentimental in art; or beautiful, pensive and enchanting in nature.[18]

The reader is increasingly struck by the parallels between Mrs West and Jane Austen, until a comparison with the equivalent passage in *Sense and Sensibility* begins to raise doubts:

> They speedily discovered that their enjoyment of dancing and music was mutual, and that it arose from a general conformity of judgment in all that related to either. Encouraged by this to a further examination of his opinions, she proceeded to question him on the subject of books; her favourite authors were brought forward and dwelt upon with so rapturous a delight, that any young man of five and twenty must have been insensible indeed, not to become an immediate convert to the excellence of such works, however disregarded before. Their taste was strikingly alike. The same books, the same passages were idolized by each – or if any difference appeared, any objection arose, it lasted no longer than till the force of her arguments and the brightness of her eyes could be displayed. He acquiesced in all her decisions, caught all her enthusiasm; and long before his visit concluded, they conversed with the familiarity of a long-established acquaintance.[19]

In no sense is this a true meeting of minds; Marianne is being deceived, and Willoughby is to some extent deceiving himself. As in *Northanger Abbey*, and once more under the guise of a literary convention and conventionality all too easily accepted by the contemporary reader, Austen is saying something more. Beneath the surface certainties lies ambiguity. As in *Northanger Abbey* we are, by a more careful reading of the text, led to question distinctions between semblance and reality. To mock at the Gothic novel was not a very original exercise, any more than it was original to decry sensibility. It must have reassured censorious readers and made publishers happy. But there are other, more disquieting messages concealed in the texts, which go some way to undermine the very certainties they appear to uphold.

Mrs West's Marianne marries her Clermont, with unhappy results, mainly due to the immaturity of Clermont and Marianne's tendency to tearful complaints. Louisa eventually marries the worthy Pelham, but before this happens the Dudley family, like the Dashwoods, suddenly find themselves poor. While Mrs West tends to stress the virtues this change of circumstances brings out in Louisa, Austen emphasises the male selfishness and legal privilege which reduces a widow and her three daughters to such circumstances.

We think of the typical courtship novel as ending on the steps of the altar, but *A Gossip's Story* is somewhat unusual in showing the deterioration of Marianne's marriage, ending in total estrangement: 'He sometimes pays a short visit to his Lady at the Park, who welcomes him with tears, and endeavours to detain him by complaints.'[20] Her over-riding reason for taking an anti-sensibility stance seems to be, not so much the difficulties which attend a young woman in search of a husband, but her trials and tribulations after she has found one. Defending the fairly trivial misunderstandings which lead to the ruin of Marianne's marriage, she writes: 'I am willing to appeal to the experience of every wedded pair, whether *great* criminality on either side is necessary, in order to render the bonds of Hymen a galling yoke of misery.'[21] We are told, mostly through Mr Dudley, that a wife should be obedient, the first to mend a quarrel, that she should respect her husband's virtues and turn a blind eye to his failings. For the modern reader Mrs West's novel is a useful corrective in our attitude to the novel of sense: it reminds us that novelists who promoted sense as opposed to romantic sensibility were as much concerned with the realities of life which awaited a girl after marriage, though these tend to be obscured by the conventions of story-telling. As Mr Dudley reminds his daughter, it is a man's qualities as a husband which matter: 'I must observe that Mr Pelham's character as a man, is of much greater consequence to your future peace, than his behaviour as a lover.' And this is a message which is explicit or implicit in all the novels of the period. It is a system of value judgements which enabled Jane Austen to dispense with great love scenes altogether. It is her lesser men, the deceivers, who are seen to behave with romantic gallantry – Willoughby, Wickham and Frank Churchill. As for Darcy, Colonel Brandon and Mr Knightley, we see them acting as gentlemen rather than as lovers, being the good landlord, the generous friend. When it comes to love, Austen imposes an almost embarrassed English restraint upon them which suits her purpose nicely. A parade of happiness is avoided, irony does not give way to sentiment, the ambiguous, self-protective shield of sense remains intact.

Hannah More's *Cœlebs in Search of a Wife* appeared in 1809, two years before Jane Austen finally appeared in print with *Sense and*

Sensibility. Closer to a didactic tract than a novel to the bemused modern reader, it is the most definitive expression of the attitudes embodied in the courtship novels of sense. Love is portrayed 'not as an ungovernable impulse, but as a sentiment arising out of qualities calculated to inspire attachment in persons under the dominion of reason and religion'.[22] The education of girls for matrimony is expatiated on at length. Mr Stanley, father of the prospective bride, proudly states:

> The inculcation of fortitude, prudence, humility, temperance, self-denial – this is education . . . . Perseverance, meekness, and industry . . . I make it a point never to extol any indications of genius . . . . Nor am I indeed over much delighted with a great blossom of talents . . . I would give every girl, in a certain station in life, some one amusing accomplishment . . . . Religion alone can counter-act the pride of talents.[23]

There are constant warnings against women who are encouraged to display their artistic accomplishments, something which was to be constantly echoed in later novels by Edgeworth:

> A woman, whose whole education has been rehearsal, will always be dull, except she lives on the stage, constantly displaying what she has been sedulously acquiring. Books on the contrary, well chosen books, do not lead to exhibition. The knowledge a woman acquires in private, desires no witness; the possession is the pleasure. It improves herself, it embellishes her family society, it entertains her husband, it informs her children. The gratification is cheap, is safe, and always to be had at home.[24]

Burney's Cecilia, Edgeworth's Belinda, Austen's Fanny Price, a great preponderance of these heroines like to devote much time to private reading. When Elizabeth Bennet plays and sings to the company she does it with a charming lack of real accomplishment, and the reason is to be found in the constant warnings against women who like to show off their accomplishments in public. As Cœlebs has been told by his father: 'you will want a COMPANION: an ARTIST you may hire'.[25]

It was one of the ironies of well-to-do society in the last decades of the eighteenth century and the beginning of the nineteenth that, having taken pride in teaching their daughters such leisure arts as piano-playing and singing at a time when it was no longer economically necessary for them to spend so much time on domestic chores, they should then have to warn young women against showing off unduly in company. One wonders to what extent these strictures were inspired by a belief in the need to exhort women to modesty, and to what extent they were simply the result of tedious hours spent listening politely in the drawing room. But of the desirable end-product of female education there was no doubt. Mr and Mrs Stanley had manufactured the perfect wife for Cœlebs:

> She enlivens without dazzling, and entertains without overpowering. Contented to please, she has no ambition to shine . . . . Of repartee she has little, and dislikes it in others. . . . Taste is indeed the predominating quality of her mind; and she may rather be said to be a nice judge of the genius of others than to be a genius herself.[26]

Maria Edgeworth was to develop the theme of the perfect wife in *Patronage*, where her heroine has all the attributes approved of by Mrs More, and who is chosen by a very distinguished man who has come to England for the specific purpose of finding himself a wife. Other female characters in the novel are contrasted with the heroine, and are particularly guilty of the vice of 'display'. They show off at every opportunity and take part in amateur theatricals, which Thomas Gisborne considered an unladylike activity in his *Duties of the Female Sex*, published in 1797. Although Austen for the most part disliked perfect heroines she was for a time influenced by the evangelical trend which Hannah More's book represented, and in *Mansfield Park*, published in the same year as *Patronage*, she did aim to create a perfect heroine with all the rather negative virtues listed in *Cœlebs*.

In a sense *Mansfield Park*, the most consciously schematic and 'evangelical' novel she ever wrote, the most devoted to Christian and conservative values, marks a turning point in Austen's writing life. Her first three books all had an element of parody, were a conscious reaction to or reaction against previous fiction, and with the parody or mimicry went a hidden ambiguity. *Sense and Sensibility* seems dogmatic and conformist enough in its treatment of poor Marianne Dashwood, who has a charm for the modern reader that the sensible

Elinor, whom Austen referred to as 'my Elinor' in her letters, can never have. But in a sense Austen avoids the real conflict of values involved in novels which extolled sense and prudence in opposition to sensibility and passion by making Marianne simply young rather than wrong-headed. As we have already seen, her meeting with Willoughby involved a good deal of self-deception and deception from the start. Like the youthful Catherine Morland, Marianne Dashwood will grow up, and in the process learn to distinguish between illusion and reality.

But there is more than irony in Marianne's ultimate marriage to Colonel Brandon; there are touches of ambiguity which suggest that Marianne has been made to 'fit', that she is the willing victim of a process of socialisation which all young girls undergo:

> Marianne Dashwood was born to an extraordinary fate. She was born to discover the falsehood of her own opinions, and to counteract, by her conduct, her most favourite maxims. She was born to overcome an affection formed so late in life as at seventeen, and with no sentiment superior to strong esteem and lively friendship, voluntarily to give her hand to another![27]

The true irony in this passage lies in the fact that Marianne Dashwood's fate is by no means 'extraordinary': most young women learnt to overcome first love, whether founded on worth or not, and settle down to marriage founded on something less than passion. And in a sense all women are 'born to discover the falsehood of their own opinions' when those opinions are at variance with the social consensus.

When we look at the closing pages we see this ambiguity confirmed by Austen's phraseology. There was, we are told, a 'confederacy against her'. Her mother's first object in life was 'to see Marianne settled at the mansion-house', a wish shared by her sister Elinor and her husband. There is a curious passivity in Austen's words as she says that '*she found herself* at nineteen, *submitting* to new attachments, entering on new duties, *placed* in a new home, a wife, the mistress of a family, and the patroness of a village'. (Author's italics). Added to the implicit passivity is the irony of the fact that at nineteen a young woman can hardly be fit for such responsibilities. Once married to a man 'whom, two years before, she had considered too old to be married', 'Marianne found her own happiness in forming his', a wifely submission which the ideal of marriage in a male-dominated society required. The modern reader tends to be shocked by the way the delightful Marianne Dashwood, so spontaneous and natural, is crushed by events and the lessons the author forces her to learn through them. It is quite possible that Austen intended to convey that sense of shock, even while apparently subscribing to the conventional dogma of sense.

Pride and Prejudice took its title from the last chapter of Burney's *Cecilia*, and also perhaps more than a hint of its hero Darcy from the Delviles, since he is quite unlike the husbands Austen normally awards her heroines: richer, grander, more aristocratic than her clergymen and modest country squires. The original title had been *First Impressions*, and it is difficult to find a didactic novel of sense which does not warn young ladies about the dangers of trusting to first impressions, but Austen's final version had been 'lop't and crop't so successfully' that the book is not only lacking in redundant information, but occasionally in that extra dimension which makes the reader understand both the characters and the moral implications of their actions more fully.[28] Austen's final version is almost too short on information, which is probably why it is read so often by people unfamiliar with the rest of Austen's work, who consider it merely a light-weight jolly romp, and read no further. The version we know relies heavily on dialogue, which suggests that this is the one thing she did not cut, but instead excised passages of authorial comment. As a result the concept of 'sense' is taken as read, in fact in this book it seems to be merely the opposite of silliness, and the convenient word 'sensible' is an all-embracing umbrella word which on this occasion conveys rather too little. It pops up with obsessive regularity, blunted by too much use. Jane says that Mr Bingley is 'sensible', the author introduces Charlotte Lucas as 'sensible'. 'Can he be a sensible man, sir?' Lizzy asks her father when Mr Collins's first letter arrives, and Mr Bennet is delighted to think he is not. Mr Bennet, the detached misanthrope, is also delighted to discover, when Charlotte accepts Mr Collins's proposal of marriage, that a woman 'whom he used to think tolerably sensible, was as foolish as his wife, and more foolish than his daughter'. Mr Gardiner, Elizabeth's uncle, is introduced as 'a sensible, gentlemanlike man' and even the youthful Miss Darcy has 'sense and good humour in her face'.

Clearly Elizabeth Bennet was intended by her creator to be that aberration of female propriety, a wit. In her quick repartee, the

underlying cynicism of her comments, she has inherited a good deal
from her father Mr Bennet, but also much from Richardson's
Charlotte Grandison, who entertains the reader, as he no doubt
entertained her creator, even while she is being rebuked by her
brother Sir Charles for her unladylike conduct. Austen, who had a
very sharp wit herself, as her letters show, was also very well aware of
the conventional attitude to wit in young ladies, but it seems to me
that she was enjoying the sparkle of her creation too much to put a
rein on her. So she left the dialogue, or perhaps even expanded it,
and reduced or cut the authorial comment with its moral pointers, so
as not to reduce the sparkle on her heroine and the sparkle of the
prose itself; because Austen, the anonymous author, was a wit, and
Elizabeth Bennet comes closest to Jane Austen herself in that respect.
It is only in the second half of the novel that the heroine is subdued,
humbled on seeing her own mistakes. And it is only now that the
author stops encouraging the reader to laugh with Mr Bennet at the
follies of his wife and daughters; now his detached cynicism is shown
as culpable negligence, though we are told that Elizabeth 'had never
been blind to the impropriety of her father's behaviour as a husband'.
And the heroine's wit and charm tend to blind the modern reader to
her more conventional aspects. She is 'spirited' enough when it
comes to Mr Collins's proposal, while her initial rejection of
Mr Darcy has its roots in literary tradition rather than unusual
character – Cecilia and Emmeline had behaved in a similar way in
similar situations. Elizabeth Bennet nevertheless subscribes to the
philosophy of 'sense' in that she has no wish to defy society: on the
contrary, she is anxious to appear in a good light in society. She is
deeply embarrassed by the behaviour of her mother and younger
sisters in public, because of the way it reflects on her, and particularly
because of the way it shames her in Darcy's eyes. She points out to
her father 'the very great disadvantage to us all, which must arise
from the public notice of Lydia's unguarded and imprudent
manner . . . '. Whereupon Mr Bennet shrewdly observes: 'What,
has she frightened away some of your lovers?' Whereupon Elizabeth
rather pompously protests: 'It is not of peculiar, but of general evils,
which I am now complaining. Our importance, our respectability in
the world must be affected by the wild volatility, the assurance and
disdain of all restraint which mark Lydia's character.'[29] And when
Lydia does elope Elizabeth is more distressed at the humiliation and
disgrace she has brought on the family, at the loss of face with regard

to Darcy whom she now wants to win, than at any possible consequences to Lydia herself. Austen certainly took more than just the title from Burney. Central to Burney's plots was the relatively humble heroine exposed to social embarrassment in the presence of her socially superior suitor, and this is a recurring theme in *Pride and Prejudice*, where appearances are also important, except that Austen makes deceptive appearances an important factor in women's assessment of men, too, so that the courtship game seems slightly less one-sided. But Darcy's proud aloofness at the ball in the assembly room is nothing to the shaming vulgarity of Mrs Bennet and the antics of her younger sisters. Elizabeth Bennet, like Evelina, has the natural good 'taste' to wish to disassociate herself from her more vulgar female relatives and to desire upward mobility through marriage. When she visits Pemberley she is accompanied by the Gardiners, who know how to behave in any company and with whom Darcy is quite at ease. Once engaged to him, she tries to keep Darcy from her relatives, except those 'with whom he might converse without mortification' and 'she looked forward with delight to the time when they should be removed from society so little pleasing to either, to all the comfort and elegance of their family party at Pemberley'.[30] Jane and Bingley soon follow them to Derbyshire: 'So near a vicinity to her mother and Meryton relations was not desirable even to *his* easy temper, or *her* affectionate heart.'[31]

These aspects of the novel, which give a rather different slant to the title, are too easily overlooked. When Elizabeth tells her aunt that she changed her mind about Darcy after seeing Pemberley we are meant to take this as a joke, but there is more than a grain of truth in the statement. The house of the prospective suitor is always an important factor in the courtship novel of this period, and the elegancies of Pemberley are no exception. Elizabeth cannot help being impressed by the scale and grandeur of the estate, and she is ruefully aware that she might have been mistress of this beautiful house and park.

Sense in the courtship novel is related to a realistic evaluation of money, something which passionate sensibility tends to ignore when it falls in love with an unsuitable object. 'Victuals and Drink' as the young Jane Austen bluntly put it, and she is equally blunt in her adult work, where we are always told exactly what each person, particularly each male suitor, is worth. Charlotte Lucas's marriage to Mr Collins, for all Elizabeth's protests and Mr Bennet's dismissive contempt, is shown by the author to be an act of rather sad, resigned good sense:

Without thinking highly either of men or of matrimony, marriage had always been her object; it was the only honourable provision for well-educated young women of small fortune, and however uncertain of giving happiness, must be their pleasantest preservative from want. This preservative she had now obtained; and at the age of twenty-seven, without ever having been handsome, she felt all the good luck of it.[32]

In *Pride and Prejudice* the polarities tend to be between sense and silliness rather than sense and sensibility. Jane and Elizabeth are sensible, i.e. intelligent, well-bred, decorous, whilst their sisters are silly, i.e. wild, uncontrolled, badly behaved, and Mary is a caricature of the unacceptable blue-stocking. Sensible Charlotte marries silly Mr Collins and makes the best of a bad job. Mr Bennet is sensible, but his wife is silly . . . or is she? We must apply Austen's own ruthless logic to the situation, and this tells us that with the family estate entailed and five dowerless daughters Mrs Bennet had ample cause to be anxious to see her daughters married off, and that her husband's amused detachment about her anxiety on what is to become of them all after his death is really the height of irresponsibility. As Elizabeth becomes a rather more thoughtful and subdued person, later in the narrative we are in fact told that she:

> had never been blind to the impropriety of her father's behaviour as a husband. She had always seen it with pain; but respecting his abilities, and grateful for his affectionate treatment of herself, she had endeavoured to forget what she could not overlook, and to banish from her thoughts that continual breach of conjugal obligation and decorum which, in exposing his wife to the contempt of her own children, was so highly reprehensible. But she never felt so strongly as now, the disadvantages which must attend the children of so unsuitable a marriage, nor ever been so fully aware of the evils arising from so ill-judged a direction of talents; talents which, rightly used, might at least have preserved the respectability of his daughters, even if incapable of enlarging the mind of his wife.[33]

Of course Mrs Bennet is a silly woman, of course she is a caricature of all the real-life mothers who were such desperate husband-hunters for their daughters, but at the same time the problems which concern her are real, and Mr Bennet is wrong to shut himself in his library and ignore them. The reader is allowed to laugh too long with Mr Bennet; perhaps because Austen 'lop't and crop't' too much, perhaps because she was carried away by her own wit, darker ambiguities are lost or diminished for the sake of surface sparkle. It is a book which is read too easily, as a gay, enjoyable love story; the stark economic realism on which the novel of sense essentially depends, and of which Austen was more sharply aware than any of her contemporaries, tends to become obscured, and with it the ambiguity which lies at the core of her early, parodic writing.

With *Mansfield Park* the element of parody and ambiguity disappears from Austen's work. Although published only a year after *Pride and Prejudice* there was in fact a considerable gap between the composition of the three early books and that of *Mansfield Park*, a decade of considerable family upheaval, including the unwelcome move to Bath, the death of her father, and a period of further uncertainty and insecurity before Jane settled at Chawton with her mother and sister. These events, particularly the death of her father and the lack, for several years, of a home they could call their own, must have helped to change Jane's attitudes considerably, and are probably responsible for the fact that house and family become a focal image for conservative values, with the father as the lynch-pin holding the whole ordered structure together.

Apart from *Northanger Abbey*, *Mansfield Park* is the only other Austen novel which takes its title from a house, and in a sense it is the antithesis of the earlier book, presenting a very different picture of patriarchal society. The house of General Tilney is founded on greed and ruled by fear: the head of the household is motivated by the desire for more money and the power it represents, he is autocratic, intimidates his own children, particularly his daughter, who is unhappy and lives in fear of him; having invited a young girl into his house he flatters her with total insincerity until he finds out that she is not the heiress he took her for, whereupon he throws her out of the house without ceremony. Sir Thomas, on the other hand, is a character whom the author regards as worthy of love and respect from his family; he is kind and benevolent; having taken young Fanny Price into his home because she is penniless, he offers her security for life. Though she is treated like a poor relation this is not the fault of the head of the household: it is partly the result of Fanny's self-effacing nature, something which has been encouraged in women, as has the unselfish goodness which makes it natural for other people in the household to exploit her. People who treat Fanny badly do so in the name of Sir Thomas, because they defer to rank with a view to improving their own insecure position, like Mrs Norris, but never with his authority. The attitude of Lady Bertram, who takes Fanny for granted but cannot be easy unless she is always in attendance, is particularly important, exposing the position of the unmarried daughter in a gentleman's family; but Fanny's visit to the dreadful home of her parents at Portsmouth provides a powerful reminder that her position at Mansfield Park, however humble, is still one to be thankful for. In addition her mother's home life provides a very unpleasant picture of the consequences of a marriage not founded on 'sense', that is, adequate resources. No leisure, no privacy, no order, no time for civilised pursuits, too many children in too little space.

Although the house is a central image in the courtship novel, Mansfield Park is not, like Pemberley, or the beautiful estate of Edgar in *Camilla*, a place to which the heroine aspires to arrive through marriage. Fanny is already in the house when the story begins, having been taken in as a child by the benign and God-like father figure, Sir Thomas, who seems to represent Christian as well as social virtues. All the children acknowledge their duty to him, even if they stray from the path of virtue in his absence; only Fanny, who is wholly good, does not, and her unflinching devotion to Sir Thomas's son and his chosen profession of the Church, which Mary Crawford scoffs at, ensures that she will never be turned away from the shelter of the patriarchal, Christian house, Mansfield Park. Fanny, though not his child, is Sir Thomas's true daughter, the one who does not stray from the ordained path of virtue, so that his own Christian charity is rewarded. By the end of the story she is no longer neglected and overlooked, but recognised for the treasure she is in the household: 'Fanny was indeed the daughter that he wanted. His charitable kindness had been rearing a prime comfort for himself. His liberality had a rich repayment . . . .'[34]

For a long time the English gentry had taken their Christian religion for granted. In most Austen novels clergymen take up their posts, and with it their assured position in society, without any need to affirm their faith through the narrative. Their Christianity is taken as read. In *Sir Charles Grandison* the model hero is asked why he never preaches a sermon, and his answer is significant:

'It would be an affront,' said Sir Charles, 'to the understanding, as well as education, of a man who took rank above a peasant, in such a country as this, to seem to question whether he *knew* his general duties or not . . .. If he should be at a loss, he *may* once a week be reminded, and his heart kept warm.'[35]

It was the kind of attitude shared, on the whole, by the Rev. George Austen and family, but by the turn of the century there was a new evangelical movement which, judging from the surviving letters, Jane Austen was inclined to take rather more seriously than her sister. And by the time she began to write *Mansfield Park* she was both an older and sadder woman: she had lost her father, shared with her widowed mother and her sister a period of insecurity without a permanent home and, had it not been for her authorship, she would have been doomed to the lot of a Fanny Price, an old maid living in obscurity, attending on her somewhat peevish invalid mother and dependent on the generosity and protection of her brothers.

The Jane Austen of the Chawton period is a very different writer from the young woman who lived at Steventon, mellower, without the fierce underlying cynicism of her earlier, parodic work. She had not only come to accept limitations, but to welcome their security. Amongst her juvenilia are some letters, fragments of yet another burlesque epistolary novel:

Tomorrow Mr. Stanly's family will drink tea with us, and perhaps the Miss Phillips will meet them. On Tuesday we shall pay Morning-Visits – On Wednesday we are to dine at Westbrook. On Thursday we have Company at home. On Friday we are to be at a private concert at Sir John Wynne's – & on Saturday we expect Miss Dawson to call in the morning, – which will complete my Daughters Introduction into Life. How they will bear so much dissipation I cannot imagine . . ..[36]

Such 'dissipation', such minor events, had of course always been the stuff of her novels, but handled not only with irony, but ambiguity. The adolescent Jane Austen seems to have been in no doubt that the limits of a daughter's education and experience were intolerably constricting, which goes some way to confirming our suspicion about the ambiguity which surrounds the reform that Marianne Dashwood undergoes between the ages of seventeen and nineteen. But the chastened Jane Austen of thirty-six had come to welcome such limits, after a decade of loss and uncertainty (reflected in the false starts of novels begun and abandoned during that time i.e. *Lady Susan* and *The Watsons*) the image of the patriarchal household and its imposed limitations represented safety, security, and order, and the children who rebel against this hierarchic patriarchal order only bring misery and disgrace upon themselves.

It is perhaps precisely because it represents a new attitude and, to some extent, a change of heart, that *Mansfield Park* is both the most schematic and overtly dogmatic of her books. One almost suspects a certain contrition in the direct and forceful way she expresses conservative attitudes she would once have used, played with, with irony, ambiguity, with tongue in cheek more often than not. And this contrition is reflected in her heroine. Fanny Price, unlike her previous heroines, is wholly good, but not in the way that conventional heroines usually were. Fanny is good in the way that traditional Christianity has required women to be good: dutiful, submissive, self-effacing. Instead of having the virtues which go to make a good wife, usually embodied in the heroine of a courtship novel, Fanny's virtues are essentially those of a dutiful daughter. A daughter of God as well as man, since it comes to the same thing. And her reward is not to escape from home through matrimony but, on the contrary, to be recognised and valued by Sir Thomas, and, by marrying Edmund, clergyman, son of God, to live always within the benign shadow of Mansfield Park. Significantly, it is the school-room, long abandoned by the Bertram sons and daughters, which Fanny makes into her private retreat. She is the only one who has been properly 'schooled', who has learnt her lessons and not forgotten them. When Sir Thomas returns unexpectedly to find the house in disorder and a performance of the scandalous play, *Lovers' Vows*, about to take place, Edmund tells his father:

> We have all been more or less to blame . . . every one of us, excepting Fanny. Fanny is the only one who has judged rightly throughout, who has been consistent.[37]

And, as the play is a microcosm of the action of the novel, the same is true of the sexual behaviour of the young people: only Fanny's judgement is right throughout, only Fanny is both correct and consistent. Maria Bertram's catastrophic behaviour is explained in terms which underline the conservative and patriarchal system of values which Mansfield Park represents:

Independence was more needful than ever . . . she was less and less able to endure the restraint which her father imposed. The liberty which his absence had given was now becoming absolutely necessary. She must escape from him and Mansfield as soon as possible, and find consolation in fortune and consequence, bustle and the world . . .. In all the important preparations of the mind she was complete, being prepared for matrimony by an hatred of home, restraint, and tranquillity; by the misery of disappointed affection, and contempt of the man she was to marry.[38]

Although other women novelists (Burney in *Camilla*, for instance) had warned against the danger of marrying simply to escape from home, the emphasis here is quite different: instead of weighing one evil against another Austen is emphasising the positive value of everything that Mansfield Park represents. 'Restraint' is a small price to pay for 'tranquillity', and Fanny Price has no doubts on that score. If she is inclined to long for more warmth and love, the visit to her family at Portsmouth sends her scurrying back to Mansfield Park with a heart full of gratitude for the benefits which have fallen to her lot. During the rehearsals of the ill-fated play, Fanny notices that 'So far from being all satisfied and all enjoying, she found every body requiring something they had not, and giving occasion of discontent to the others.'[39] Fanny, on the other hand, is content with what life and Sir Thomas have given her, and devotes herself to smoothing out other people's problems.

Since Fanny's characteristics represent the essence of what Christianity and a male-dominated society required of woman, particularly the woman who did not marry and remained at home, *Mansfield Park* represents not just a novel of 'sense' in the usual sense, but sense internalised, and in that sense the novel is very unusual, since most novels preached sense as a form of necessary prudence, given the kind of society into which women were born, and the dogma of sense was little more than a didactic veneer. So there is some truth in the odd comment in a letter of Jane to her sister: 'Mr Cooke says "it is the most sensible novel he ever read", and the manner in which I treat the clergy delights them very much.'

Fanny comes to Mansfield Park as a child, and in a sense she never really grows up. She remains a dutiful child, with little or no sexuality, and her marriage to Edmund seems little more than a device to wind up the story in a conventional manner, whilst keeping her close to Mansfield Park and Sir Thomas. Most 'good' heroines of the period were paragons of beauty, demure, modest, but with all the attributes designed to make a man happy and win the heroine an honoured place in the stakes of matrimony. Fanny Price has none of those attributes. If Jane Eyre represents Charlotte Brontë's passionate rebellion at the doom of the woman who has little or no hope of winning in those stakes, Fanny Price represents Austen's reasoned resignation at the same fate: resignation which becomes positive acceptance through a scheme of values which endorses the patriarchal household as a microcosm of a greater order.

Mansfield Park is not only a change from Austen's previous work in being unambiguous in its intentions, she also hammers home the message in a way which is very unusual for her. We are given not only the microcosmic incident of the young people preparing to perform the play during the absence of Sir Thomas, but the visit to the mansion at Sotherton, which fulfills the same function even more explicitly. The young people carry on their dangerous flirtations, explore the 'wilderness', and Maria Bertram, flirting with Henry and complaining that 'unluckily that iron gate, that ha-ha, gives me a feeling of restraint' slips through the railings with him, thus symbolising her future elopement. Meanwhile Fanny's tussle with Mary Crawford over Edmund's profession is reflected in their visit to the chapel and their discussion on family prayers. 'There is something in a chapel and chaplain so much in character with a great house, with one's ideas of what such a household should be!' exclaims Fanny, reflecting her author's own vision of Mansfield Park, while Mary dismisses the notion as a charade of hypocrisy.[40] It is also Mary Crawford who, not knowing the absent Sir Thomas, comments rather sarcastically on the respect he seems to command, whereupon she is told:

> You will find his consequence very just and reasonable when you see him in his family, I assure you. I do not think we do so well without him. He has a fine dignified manner, which suits the head of such a house, and keeps every body in their place.[41]

Humble Fanny Price always knows her place, and accepts it without resentment, even gratitude. In a sense such a posture is only tenable within a specifically Christian ethic of pre-ordained hierarchy, something that Austen, with her sharply logical mind, obviously understood.

Houses and the father–daughter relationship also play a very important part in *Emma*, where some of the values so positively expressed in *Mansfield Park* are still present in a less explicit form, but combined with, one might even say reconciled with, the more conventional aims of the courtship novel.

Emma as a heroine is the very opposite of Fanny Price. If Fanny is Austen's most humble heroine, Emma is by far the most exalted one in terms of rank and fortune that Austen ever created. Fanny is penniless and adopted in the household of Sir Thomas Bertram, whilst Emma is an heiress and already rules over the house which she will one day own. Both women are dutiful daughters, but in very different ways: while Fanny looks up to Sir Thomas's wise authority Emma is always patiently considerate of her father's obvious foolishness. Fanny suffers from lack of confidence, whilst Emma's fault is that she has far too much. Few people ask Fanny's opinion or advice, for the most part she watches in silence, knowing that other people's judgement is wrong whilst hers is right. Emma regards herself as a fount of wisdom and authority, entitled to redirect other people's lives, and she is almost invariably wrong.

It is as though, in *Emma*, Austen has taken the values so explicitly stated in *Mansfield Park*, and given them a further dimension, that of freedom of choice. And imaginative use of existential freedom of choice within a framework of conservative values gives the novel an extraordinary naturalism and balance. Because Fanny Price, for all her pious submission, to God, to duty, to Sir Thomas and his family, has very little freedom of choice; straying beyond the imposed limits of Mansfield Park would bring poverty and disgrace. It is only by accepting the caste system and her own humble place in it that she is herself acceptable. But Emma is in a very different social position: she is an heiress, and has an assured social position. She has been allowed a considerable degree of personal freedom from an early age, and has enough wit and beauty to scoff at matrimony as a goal for herself: 'A single woman with a very narrow income must be a ridiculous, disagreeable old maid . . . but a single woman of good fortune is always respectable, and may be as sensible and pleasant as anybody else.'[42] She discharges her duties as a village patroness with sense and compassion, and gives the impression of being older than her years. But Emma, from choice, always puts her father first. As his only remaining daughter still at home she is endlessly considerate, wonderfully patient with his old-womanish fads. Mr Woodhouse is not only the antithesis of Sir Thomas, but the very opposite of the wise father-figures which haunt women's fiction at this period, spouting words of wisdom to daughters on the threshold of life. He is frail, silly and tiresome, an old person who sees little beyond his own physical needs, and whose anxiety for other people is based not on superior wisdom but pettish selfishness. His belief that no woman could leave Hartfield and be happy is a comic delusion.

Nevertheless Emma tells Knightley that she cannot marry while her father is alive, and Knightley resolves the problem by offering to live at Hartfield during her father's lifetime, which Emma recognises as a considerable sacrifice on his part, since Donwell is the first house in the neighbourhood. Both Emma and Knightley display in abundance those qualities which Austen had always associated with conservative values but had never explored with such naturalness and conviction before: qualities of unselfishness, consideration and kindness. When the repentant Marianne Dashwood tells her sister: 'I cannot express my abhorrence of myself. Whenever I looked towards the past, I saw some duty neglected, or some failing indulged' and promises to 'practise the civilities, the lesser duties of life, with gentleness and forbearance'[43] one feels she has learnt a theoretical lesson by rote; it is light years away from Emma's shame at her treatment of Miss Bates, or the real goodness of her gentle treatment of Mr Woodhouse. And the same is true of the male characters. We are told that Colonel Brandon is a sensible man, but we can see for ourselves that Knightley is. We are told that Darcy is a good landlord, and assume the same of Brandon, but in *Emma* Austen actually shows us the good squire at home: we see Mr Knightley's relationship with his tenant farmer, and his practical concern about crops and the use of his land.

Emma lacks the underlying ambiguity of the three early novels, and their parodic element. If Mr Knightley is related to the mentor suitors of past courtship novels it has ceased to matter, because of Austen's natural artistry in this novel. If Emma comes from a long line of female characters who have been 'indulged' in their youth, it is also irrelevant, because of what Austen makes of her. The concept of good sense is not narrowly related to prudence and propriety, but broadened out to a set of social values within a traditional community truthfully described. Nor does Austen avoid the issue of the position of women in that conventional society by making her heroine a rich woman. There are plenty of female characters in the novel – Miss

Bates, Jane Fairfax and Harriet Smith – to remind the reader that Emma's position is one of unusual privilege, and Emma herself is intelligent enough to know it. Emma herself values openness and candour in social dealing, and this was in the tradition of the novel of sense, which constantly warned against secret dealings with male suitors, particularly secret engagements or elopements, as ultimately damaging to the woman herself. But Emma, considering Jane Fairfax's secret engagement, forgives it because the penniless Jane Fairfax was doomed to become a governess: 'If a woman can ever be excused for thinking only of herself, it is in a situation like Jane Fairfax's.'[44] When Emma considered that the duties of a governess 'seemed, under the most favourable circumstances, to require something more than human perfection of body and mind to be discharged with tolerable comfort' she found it 'impossible to feel anything but compassion and respect'.[45]

Thus, in *Emma*, not only Austen, but her characters, are aware that the ideal behaviour required of women by society, and reflected in women's fiction, had realistic limits. There is a flash of true Austen irony in the statement that the position of governess required 'something more than human perfection', since it was no less than human perfection which society required of women, an idealised perfection so often reflected in the heroines of fiction. If Emma, with all her natural and social advantages, could and should endeavour to correct her faults, to fit in with the wishes of others, to be unselfish and considerate, thus strengthening the social fabric of which she was a part, it was expecting too much of the Jane Fairfaxes of the world to behave in the same way.

If *Emma* lacks the cynical ambiguity of the early novels it also lacks the schematic dogmatism of *Mansfield Park*, which marked an important turning point in her writing career. The young Jane Austen who had been so sharp about the tedious social limits of a young woman's life had become the mature author who could write to her niece Anna, trying her hand at novel-writing: 'You are now collecting your People delightfully, getting them exactly into such a spot as is the delight of my life; – 3 or 4 Families in a Country Village is the very thing to work on.'[46] And that delight, once settled at Chawton, after the uneasy years at Bath and Southampton, clearly went beyond fictional purposes. *Emma* radiates a contentment with English country life, a love of solid English virtues and a tolerance of its foibles.

Of course, up to a point the pro-English stance belonged to the novel of sense anyhow. We have seen how English women novelists contrasted English sense, and their own didactic fiction, with the romantic sensibility and sexual licence associated with foreign fiction. Edgeworth in particular, having travelled abroad, made a point of contrasting English and French social mores with regard to courtship and marriage. In *Patronage* she presents a heroine who has all the virtues associated with the ideal companionate marriage: she is educated, but with no wish to outshine a husband; beautiful but modest; and although accomplished and cultivated does not despise domestic duties. Her foreign suitor has come to England to find an English wife; as for the false gallantry of the French, it was almost a cliché in fiction. Mr Knightley's Englishness suits Austen very well, since he does not have to be passionate. But one feels that her emphasis on the qualities of England in this book is genuinely felt, and a very long way indeed from the irony of *Northanger Abbey*, with its ambiguous pro-English speeches.

Persuasion appeared after Austen's death in 1818, and it reads like the epitaph to an era, but also seems like a personal recantation of the assumed philosophy of sense and prudence which Austen, along with her contemporaries, had preached for so long. 1818 was also the year in which Mary Shelley's *Frankenstein* first appeared, a work of female imagination which, far from accepting the status quo of a male-dominated and male-created society, condemned it utterly as a monstrous aberration, destructive and unnatural. Times were changing, and a younger literary generation was finding inspiration in the German and French literature which Austen's generation loved to hate. Insular Burkean conservatism had lost all conviction as a tide of new ideas swept to English shores, and upper-class ladies preaching prudence and control sounded absurd in that thunder.

It has been suggested that Austen's *Persuasion* is markedly different from her previous work because of a change in fashion, a trend towards greater subjectivity in narration, for instance. I find such an argument unconvincing. The sad autumnal quality of the novel is so pervasive, the efforts to justify Anne Elliot's youthful refusal of Wentworth in terms of sense and prudence are so feeble in comparison to the overwhelming mood of regret, that one can only conclude that the author is reassessing the philosophy of sense so forcefully fed to the young women readers of her day, and that she finds it sadly inadequate. It must also be remembered that while she was writing *Persuasion* she was already a sick woman, dying of a disease which in those days had no name and must have seemed sinister and mysterious. Under such circumstances the melancholy shades of autumn, the constant references to ageing and decay, the sad heroine whose 'bloom . . . vanished early' and who is 'faded and thin' are hardly surprising.

For whatever reason, the tone of regret is unmistakable. Austen's philosophy of sense was always linked to the idea of unselfishness, but in *Persuasion* this logic begins to look suspiciously like self-delusion. The sad heroine tries to console herself with the fact that 'It was not merely selfish caution, under which she acted . . . . Had she not imagined herself consulting his good, even more than her own, she could hardly have given him up.'[47] But of course events have proved her wrong, she simply *imagined* she was acting for the best, when in fact she was the victim of persuasion from an authority figure, the older woman who preached sense and prudence:

> How eloquent could Anne Elliot have been, – how eloquent, at least, were her wishes on the side of early warm attachment, and a cheerful confidence in futurity, against that over-anxious caution which seems to insult exertion and distrust Providence! – She had been forced into prudence in her youth, and she learned romance as she grew older.[48]

And how eloquent the sick and faded Jane Austen has suddenly become on the side of early warm attachment and romance, now that her middle-aged future looks so bleak. The 'desolate tranquillity' of the sad, faded Anne Elliot, longing for 'the influence so sweet and so sad of the autumnal months in the country' is light years away from the robust confidence of the Emma Woodhouse created just before she became ill, a heroine who pictured herself as a happy spinster finding just enough emotional support in her nephews and nieces.

The intimations of mortality that go with autumn are strong in *Persuasion*. Sir Walter Elliott is a fool:

> for thinking himself and Elizabeth as blooming as ever, amidst the wreck of the good looks of every body else; for he could plainly see how old all the rest of his family and acquaintances were growing.

Anne haggard, Mary coarse, every face in the neighbourhood worsting; and the rapid increase of the crow's foot about Lady Russell's temples had long been a distress to him.[49]

The overheard lecture of Captain Wentworth on firmness of character which resists persuasion, his exemplar of 'a beautiful glossy nut, which, blessed with original strength, has outlived all the storms of autumn' is itself an image of nature, and thus subject to natural decay, and there is something oddly ambiguous in the way he finishes his lecture: 'My first wish for all, whom I am interested in, is that they should be firm. If Louisa Musgrove would be beautiful and happy in her November of life, she will cherish all her present powers of mind.'[50] Given the imagery, the reader cannot help feeling that it is not altogether within the power of Louisa to cherish all her present powers in old age, any more than it is in the power of the hazel nut to be one of those with 'not a weak spot any where' and endure, 'while so many of its brethren have fallen and been trodden under foot'.

Anne's faded looks are contrasted to the appearance of Wentworth who, if anything, has grown handsomer with time. The feeling that time deals more harshly with women, that they age faster and that this is at least partly due to the restricted lives they lead, pervades the book. The elderly Mrs Croft is robust and vigorous because she chose a different path from Anne, marrying her nautical husband after a very quick courtship and sharing the hardships of his life. Austen irony runs in an unusual direction when Mrs Croft says of her courtship: 'if Miss Elliot were to hear how soon we came to an understanding, she would never be persuaded that we could be happy together.'[51] And this comes at the conclusion of the walk where Anne hears Wentworth lecture Louisa Musgrove on the hardy hazel nut and then he places the fatigued Anne Elliott in the Crofts' chaise for a lift home. Comparing the situation of the bereaved Captain Benwick to her own Anne thinks: 'I cannot believe his prospects so blighted for ever. He is younger than I am; younger in feeling, if not in fact; younger as a man. He will rally again, and be happy with another.'[52] With the hope of renewal and a second chance Anne's youthful good looks return, but there was to be no renewal for the author of *Persuasion*. In the words of her sister, 'She wrote whilst she could hold a pen, and with a pencil when a pen was become too laborious'[53] and died on 18 July 1817.

7. The Suppressed Self

THERE is a gap of almost thirty years between the death of Jane Austen and the sudden eruption, in 1847, of the Brontë sisters on the English literary scene. As far as women's fiction was concerned it was a curiously disappointing period, even though their professional status as writers was more secure than it had ever been. There were historical novels, following the success of Scott's *Waverley* novels, and romances of high society, rather pedestrian bread-and-butter stuff. The work of the widowed Mary Shelley is particularly disappointing after her astonishing debut with *Frankenstein*. It suggests that Shelley's encouragement was crucial to the production of that work, and that without his guidance she lost all real sense of literary purpose.

In England the main impetus of the romantic movement came through poetry, and here women stood very much on the sidelines, living through men who could give them some kind of vicarious freedom. Dorothy Wordsworth, Mary Shelley, even Lady Caroline Lamb, all wrote prose under the shadow of those free male spirits who could somehow endorse their lack of convention while the women themselves never ceased to look up to their male genius, the glory of which reflected on them. At this time there was no tradition of female poetry in which the new spirit could have found a voice, and the old prose model of the conservative courtship novel had not been replaced by anything more appropriate.

But there was also a more fundamental problem as far as women's writing was concerned. Romanticism had to do with a new freedom of the spirit, with individualism and self-expression, and this was a stumbling block for women. Even though politically the literary avant-garde might favour sexual equality the reality of women's lives was very different, as Mary Shelley's life with Shelley, admirer of Godwin and Wollstonecraft, amply shows. While Shelley sings lyrically of free love Mary is sadly silent about the misery of her many pregnancies far from home. As for freedom of spirit, self-expression of the individual, how could women even begin to voice such sentiments at a time when economic, psychological and sexual constraints were overpowering? The few women who did align themselves totally with the new values tended to become victims. One thinks of Mary Wollstonecraft's unhappy love life, the lives of Mary Shelley and Claire Clairmont, Wordsworth's Annette Vallon. To live such a life involved shame, heartache and illegitimate children: to have promoted such ideals intellectually or imaginatively would have been the height of irresponsibility even if it had been possible.

It was not remotely possible for women to express themselves through fiction in terms of free individualism, because they were not free. To a great extent the social restraints had been internalised, and even those women who were sufficiently intelligent to question social restraints on women had other restraints imposed on them: the restraints of life as it is, which reality imposes on all writers; the restraints of a commercial publishing system which would reject reflections on and of the world too far from the general consensus.

But sooner or later the subjective voice of woman was bound to make itself heard. Internal and external constraints ensured that it was expressed with a certain degree of disguise and subterfuge. Sometimes the voice does not know quite what it is saying, or does not wish to know. That the tone was one of anger and grievance, under the circumstances, was inevitable. The blithe and soaring spirit of the skylark belonged to man; woman was earthbound and far from happy.

One way to avoid the disturbing demands of the inner voice is to channel literary invention into 'objective' social comment. This is what Harriet Martineau did, using her considerable talent in stories designed to be *Illustrations of Political Economy* which were highly successful and gained her considerable power and influence as a pamphleteer. It is interesting to note that, although she researched many trades and professions, she never chose to illustrate the laws of political economy which oppressed women both as wives and wage-earners. One must assume a conscious or subconscious avoidance, particularly in view of the fact that Martineau never married, and worked tremendously hard at her writing to support herself and her mother.

In 1839, several years after the successful *Illustrations of Political Economy*, Martineau published *Deerbrook*, a novel which shows that she could have become a novelist of considerable importance. It also reveals glimpses of a view of womanhood so painful that her previous avoidance of the novel, her lifelong choice of objectivity through journalism, becomes understandable.

In some ways *Deerbrook* looks forward to George Eliot. Its social
setting is middle-class, a feature which was sufficiently unfashionable
at a time when literary interest was for novels of high society or
Dickensian working class to prompt the publisher John Murray to
turn it down. Martineau skilfully blends the personal lives of two
sisters with social comment and analysis of the village in which they
come to live. The village is portrayed as a hive of gossip, rumour and
personal rivalries, highly destructive in their effects. Margaret goes to
live with her sister Hester when the latter marries the local doctor,
who is ostracised and brought to the brink of ruin when he refuses to
vote for the squire's man in a local election. The doctor is portrayed
as a figure of liberal enlightenment and good will who is up against
ignorance and superstition as well as disease; his house is attacked,
but his selfless devotion during a killing epidemic redeems his place in
the community.

The emotional lives of the two sisters are played out against this
strong social background. The doctor is in fact in love with Margaret,
but marries Hester out of a misguided sense of honour. The portrayal
of Hester is a curious and interesting one, since she begins as a rather
pettish character, full of faults which disappear as life becomes more
difficult; as her husband's difficulties increase, as their household
becomes more impoverished and outside hostilities increase, she
gradually gains in courage and firmness, till she positively glows with
pride and achievement, and her husband no longer regrets that he
married the 'wrong' sister. Adversity is shown as a positive learning
experience.

But the central character is the younger sister, Margaret, who is in
love with Philip. Margaret befriends an impoverished and crippled
young woman, Maria, who lives alone, ekes out a penurious
existence as a non-resident governess to local children, and has, since
an accident made her lame, given up all hopes of marriage. Once she
herself had hopes of marrying Philip, and she is still trying to stifle her
secret passion for him when she becomes the friend and confidante of
Margaret. At the heart of the book are conversations between Maria
and Margaret on woman's lot – on love, marriage, the pain of
undeclared love, the difficulty of earning a living – which could have
been written by Charlotte Brontë and undoubtedly led her to express
such great admiration for the book, both to its author and to others.

We know that Charlotte Brontë identified with heroines who
seemed destined to be excluded from love and passion, women who
were plain, obscure and poor, but it is perhaps a surprise to find

Harriet Martineau creating an eloquent forerunner for Jane Eyre in Maria Young. But while Jane seethes with secret rebellion Maria has reached a plateau of philosophic resignation. In *Shirley* Charlotte Brontë would expatiate at some length on the secret humiliation of a woman suffering from unrequited love, since social custom demands that a woman must only respond to male advances. Martineau, through Maria Young, understands the problem but sees a salvation in suffering:

> There are no bounds to the horror, disgust and astonishment expressed when a woman owns her love to an object unasked . . . . No woman can endure the bare thought of the case being her own; and this proves the strong natural and educational restraint under which we all lie: but I must think that the frequent and patient endurance proves a strength of soul, a vigour of moral power, which ought to console and animate us in the depth of our abasement, if we could but recall it then when we want support and solace most.[1]

But there is more to this discussion than the misery of a woman's unspoken love. Maria suggests that all women are quite unprepared for love, and must suffer when it comes. Marriage, she says, is something which girls think of as 'something which will give them money, and ease, and station, and independence from their parents. This has nothing to do with love.' Love, she goes on, 'the grand influence of a woman's life, but whose name is a mere empty sound to her till it becomes, suddenly, secretly, a voice which shakes her being to the very centre' brings 'the agony of a change of existence which must be wrought without any eye perceiving it . . . . The struggles of shame, the pangs of despair, must be hidden in the depths of the prison-house.'

Martineau is writing about sexual passion, which for a woman was associated with shame and secrecy, a secret revolutionary change between girlhood and womanhood for which her upbringing in no way prepared her. Worse: there was a conspiracy of silence between women, between mothers and daughters, because of social and internalised restraints, so that each woman, when the crisis point comes, suffers alone, believing herself in some way unique:

> Every mother and friend hopes that no one else has suffered as she did – that her particular charge may escape entirely, or get off

more easily. Then there is the shame of confession which is involved: some conclude, at a distance of time, that they may have exaggerated their own sufferings, or have been singularly rebellious and unreasonable. Some lose the sense of the anguish in the subsequent happiness; and there are not a few who, from constitution of mind, forget altogether 'the things that are behind.' When you remember, too, that it is the law of nature and providence that each should bear his and her own burden, and that no warning would be of any avail, it seems no longer so strange that while girls hear endlessly of marrriage, they are kept wholly in the dark about love.

But there is more involved in the tortured and circuitous path from girlhood to womanhood than the secret shock of sexuality. Martineau writes that 'some conclude, at a distance of time, that they may have exaggerated their own sufferings, or have been singularly rebellious and unreasonable'. The *rite de passage* from girlhood to womanhood involved a breaking of the spirit, a crushing of the tomboy, of the active ego, in order to produce a modest, submissive adult woman. The mature Jane Austen rather carefully avoided describing young girls: in 1814 she wrote to her niece Anna that 'till the heroine grows up, the fun must be imperfect . . .. One does not care for girls till they are grown up', but in her youthful *Northanger Abbey* she describes the child Catherine Morland as a tomboy who did not conform to the female ideal at all:

She was fond of all boys' plays, and greatly preferred cricket not merely to dolls, but to the more heroic enjoyments of infancy, nursing a dormouse, feeding a canary-bird, or watering a rosebush. Indeed she had no taste for a garden; and if she gathered flowers at all, it was chiefly for the pleasure of mischief . . . she was moreover noisy and wild, hated confinement and cleanliness, and loved nothing so well in the world as rolling down the green slope at the back of the house.[2]

The transformation of Catherine Morland between the ages of ten and fifteen is relatively painless. Mrs Morland is a good woman who, with a large brood of younger children, leaves Catherine to run wild. Her childhood is happy, and the heroine's pain and disillusion waits for her in the outside world. Austen, like so many of her contemporaries, seems to have found a sense of social and emotional security within her own family. Later women writers, coming from a lower socio-economic group in which the family did not offer a lifelong security, but, on the contrary, used and exploited its womenfolk whilst investing all its limited resources on male offspring, saw early life in terms of struggle and rebellion.

The misery, rebellion and rage of childhood was to become an important feature in the novels of Victorian women writers. This was another point of affinity between Charlotte Brontë and Harriet Martineau who, when she read *Jane Eyre*, felt that the author must have known about parts of her own childhood, whilst Brontë, when she read the parts of *Household Education* which related to Martineau's own childhood, felt that it was like meeting her own double.

Although *Deerbrook* begins when the heroine is already grown-up, there is one reference to her childhood which sounds suspiciously autobiographical and which foreshadows the spirit of Jane Eyre, Catherine Earnshaw and, come to that, Maggie Tulliver in the *Mill on the Floss*:

> Margaret was, for an hour or two, possessed with the bad spirit of defiance. Her mind sank back into what it had been in her childhood, when she had hidden herself in the lumber-room, or behind the water-tub, for many hours, to make the family uneasy, because she had been punished – in the days when she bore every infliction that her father dared to try, with apparent unconcern, rather than show to watchful eyes that she was moved, – in the days when the slightest concession would dissolve her stubbornness in an instant, but when, to get rid of a life of contradiction, she had had serious thoughts of cutting her throat, had gone to the kitchen door to get the carving-knife, and had been much disappointed to find the servants at dinner, and the knife-tray out of reach.[3]

This is a very different view of the patriarchal family from that put forward by an earlier generation of women writers. The wise protective father figure is punitive, forces his daughter into 'a life of contradiction' and rouses in her 'the bad spirit of defiance'.

These contradictions inevitably affected women writers themselves, who could only find expression for these inner storms, which were also shameful, in a veiled way. The internalisation of restraints could mean that the author herself was only half aware of the import and inner drive of her fiction. This certainly seems to have been the case with Charlotte Brontë. As for Harriet Martineau, the odd little revelation quoted above, which seems to have nothing to do with the narrative flow of the novel, and even less relevance to the well-adjusted nature of the heroine, tends to confirm the suspicion that Martineau may indeed have escaped into objectivity in fictional pamphleteering, even if the 'coming to terms' reflected in the philosophical resignation of Maria Young was genuine enough.

The contradiction of opposing forces was very strong in Charlotte Brontë. Anger and resentment at her woman's lot were in conflict with her Christian piety and her passionate hunger for love. The object of her desire was also the oppressor, and her sexual passion was doubly shameful because its object was unlawful. The outcome was conscious denial and suppression, resulting in powerful subconscious expression through myth. Charlotte Brontë was equipped to take this way out: from childhood she and her brother and sisters had been creating a fanciful alternative world in the stories of Angria, which continued right through her adolescence to the time she came to Brussels. And she wrote in a trance-like state, with her eyes closed, a manner of composition which not only heightened her inner visions by shutting out the real world but gave maximum encouragement to the voice of the subconscious. When stories tell themselves, or are allowed to tell themselves with only a minimum interference from the conscious critical faculty, they tend to have a deeper, inner meaning of which the author is only partly aware. In the case of Charlotte Brontë her fiction became a powerful safety valve for conflicting fires which erupted like a hidden volcano.

In this respect a letter she wrote to G. H. Lewes in January 1848 is revealing. Lewes had written to her in terms of admiration after the publication of *Jane Eyre*, but nevertheless took it upon himself to recommend her to read Jane Austen. Brontë did so, and was unimpressed, and with considerable insight described her work as 'a carefully-fenced, highly cultivated garden',[4] and for the rest of her life she continued to be less than enthusiastic about Austen's work because of her deliberate exclusion of passion and strong feelings. In this particular letter to Lewes she is receptive to his warning against 'melodrama' and promises to 'endeavour to follow the counsel which shines out of Miss Austen's "mild eyes," "to finish more and be more subdued;" ' but she cannot be sure of doing any such thing. She recognises the trance-like compulsion of her work:

When authors write best, or, at least, when they write most fluently, an influence seems to waken in them, which becomes their master – which will have its own way – putting out of view all behests but its own, dictating certain words, and insisting on their being used, whether vehement or measured in their nature; new-moulding characters, giving unthought of turns to incidents, rejecting carefully-elaborated old ideas, and suddenly creating and adopting new ones.

Written after the successful publication of *Jane Eyre*, this is no doubt an accurate description of its composition as the author saw it, one which our analysis will tend to confirm. But when she first wrote back to Lewes in November 1847 she defended herself by referring back to an earlier composition, *The Professor*, which had failed to find a publisher:

You warn me to beware of melodrama, and you exhort me to adhere to the real. When I first began to write, so impressed was I with the truth of the principles you advocate, that I determined to take Nature and Truth as my sole guides . . . I restrained imagination, eschewed romance, repressed excitement; over-bright colouring too, I avoided, and sought to produce something which should be soft, grave and true.[5]

In other words she wrote it, not in a trance-like state, eyes shut, but with her eyes wide open to the outside, 'real' world which she clearly conceives to be dull and grey in comparison to her interior world. And then her use of words is significant: she '*restrained* imagination, *eschewed* romance, *repressed* excitement' making it obvious that to depict her calm, cool outer world she was having actively to repress some inner fire. Why?

There is nothing in her literary development to suggest that Charlotte Brontë ever developed literary theories which favoured cool realism. Family reading at Haworth definitely seems to have favoured the wild and romantic, including supernatural stories from the *Methodist Magazine*, and the continuing saga of Angria is certainly a Gothic fantasy. When introduced to Austen she said she preferred George Sand. Of course, up to a point it was natural that she should turn away from Angria as a form of protracted adolescent fantasy, particularly if she was to succeed in the real world as a publishable novelist. In an exercise book kept at Brussels she jotted down notes for a possible novel: it was to be set in England 'from 30–50 years ago', to be rural, middle-class, narrated in the first person, with a plot described as 'Domestic – the romantic note excluded'. The problem of her own female anger and resentment was clearly recognised: her final note being 'No grumbling allowed'.[6]

Before embarking on *The Professor* she did jot down a 'Farewell to Angria' couched in typical imagery:

> 'I long to quit for a while the burning clime where we have sojourned too long – its skies flame – the glow of sunset is always upon it – the mind would cease from excitement and turn now to a cooler region where the dawn breaks grey and sober, and the coming day for a time at least is subdued by clouds.[7]

Charlotte Brontë's imagery is obsessive and ultimately self-revealing, and the cool grey skies which hang over the scenes of *The Professor* are not only in sharp contrast to the juvenilia, but to the glaring sunsets which constantly illuminate the wilder scenes of *Jane Eyre*. *The Professor* represents not only a misguided false start into professional authorship, it is also a temporary distortion from her true literary bent as a result of her traumatic experience in Brussels.

As Martineau's *Deerbrook* makes clear, women were unprepared, through upbringing, to cope with the first shock of sexual love. When it came, it was something shameful, to be hidden from the outside world and even from oneself. 'Female delicacy', social and psychological constraints made it out of the question for a woman to reveal any feeling for a man unasked, unless he had already declared himself in love with her. But if there was a shame even greater than that of betraying unrequited passion, it was for that object to be unlawful. Brontë, in love with the married M. Heger, concealed the truth from herself, deluded herself into believing that it was simply a master–pupil relationship, one which male-dominated society endorsed in both life and fiction. When Madame Heger revealed the truth to her, her reaction was one of anger, hatred and denial.

The denial of sexual passion continued in the writing of *The Professor*, which dealt with the Brussels episode. It is usually seen as a form of wish-fulfilment, but that came later, hidden and disguised in *Jane Eyre*. In *The Professor* she is sticking to her conscious, intellectual cover story, that her feeling for the professor was pure and asexual, based on an affinity of spirit. The fact that it is reciprocated in the same fashion, that she is his chosen pupil, is the only element of wish-fulfilment.

Except when she wrote *Shirley*, where she was consciously trying to get away from the subjective voice and broaden her scope to take in social themes and problems, Charlotte Brontë always chose a first person narrator. All the Brontës did, and it is an important, one could even say, revolutionary, element in their work. But *The Professor* is the only novel in which Charlotte Brontë chose a male narrator, and she is so ill at ease with him that one is forced to conclude that she chose Crimsworth as a narrator to put as great a distance between herself as author and the female heroine, with all the painful dangers that would entail. And Crimsworth himself is a rather cold character.

Images associated with heat were to have important sexual connotations in Charlotte Brontë's later work, and these are not simply lacking in *The Professor*: they have been replaced by cold images. Cold grey skies are as much a feature of this book as fiery sunsets are a feature of *Jane Eyre*. And the fiercely Protestant ethic which runs through the book is associated not just with hard work and endeavour, but with sexual purity.

Charlotte Brontë links her hero and heroine spiritually by making both of them Protestants in a country where everybody else is Roman Catholic. Their relationship is curiously asexual, in fact Crimsworth admires Frances Henri for her modest purity and lack of sexual intent. This is in strong contrast to the other, Roman Catholic, girls in the school, who Crimsworth as narrator describes in the following, unflattering terms:

> They were each and all supposed to have been reared in utter unconsciousness of vice. The precautions to keep them ignorant, if not innocent, were innumerable. How was it, then, that scarcely one of those girls having attained the age of fourteen could look a man in the face with modesty and propriety? An air of bold, impudent flirtation, or a loose, silly leer, was sure to answer the most ordinary glance from a masculine eye . . . these girls belonged to what are called the respectable ranks of society; they had all been carefully brought up, yet was the mass of them mentally depraved.[8]

Such fierce charges of depravity usually go with the denial of any such impulses in oneself, and are too irrational not to seem suspect. Of course the headmistress of this school, the Madame Heger of the story, is a Catholic, and Crimsworth had at first been attracted to her, before learning to detest her. When Frances Henri appears on the scene she is just as vehemently anti-Catholic, and her Swiss father and English mother seem a convenient device for making her so. When she tells Crimsworth of her longing to get to England she does so in terms suggestive of the 'spying' Madame Heger:

> I long to live once more among Protestants; they are more honest than Catholics; a Romish school is a building with porous walls, a hollow floor, a false ceiling; every room in this house, Monsieur, has eye-holes and ear-holes, and what the house is, the inhabitants are, very treacherous; they all think it lawful to tell lies; they call it politeness to profess friendship where they feel hatred.[9]

This passage is full of her hatred for Madame Heger, who had absolutely no reason to fear for her own marriage and simply suggested that Charlotte was in love with her husband and should, therefore, leave the school and return to England in her own best interest.

In *The Professor* Zoraïde Reuter dismisses Frances Henri because she is jealous of Crimsworth's interest in the girl. But he is interested in her because she is a good pupil. When she writes essays he is interested not just in her style, but the sentiments which she expresses, imbued with the spirit of self-help and dogged self-reliance. When she writes an essay on a New World emigrant:

> Mdlle. Henri failed not to render audible the voice of resolve, patience, endeavour. The disasters which had driven him from his native country were alluded to: stainless honour, inflexible independence, indestructible self-respect there took the word.[10]

This reflects both the attitude and circumstances which led Crimsworth to leave England and make his own way in the world. When he finds Frances again it is in the Protestant cemetery; when he makes her his wife it is more as a partner in a life of hard work and endeavour than anything else.

In her preface Charlotte Brontë reveals that she made a conscious decision about the kind of hero she wished to create:

> I said to myself that my hero should work his way through life as I had seen real living men work theirs – that he should never get a

shilling he had not earned . . . that he should not even marry a
beautiful girl or a lady of rank. As Adam's son he should share
Adam's doom, and drain throughout life a mixed and moderate
cup of enjoyment.

Names of characters are always important in Charlotte Brontë's
novels, and Crimsworth certainly suggests the penny-pinching
Yorkshire millowner's family from which he comes. Of course, in
another sense Crimsworth is not so much sharing 'Adam's doom' as
that of Eve: she has created a hero who is as humble as the heroine, as
poor as the author herself.

But for Charlotte Brontë in this book the Protestant ethic of hard
work and endeavour is essentially devoid of joy. She may speak of a
'moderate cup of enjoyment' but her vision is rather more bleak. She
is not just being anti-romantic in a literary sense, she seems to be
curbing her own inner visions of hope and passion, the fiery climes of
Angria, in order to face the bleak light of common day. Chapter 19 of
The Professor, a key chapter of the novel, begins with a little lecture:

> Novelists should never allow themselves to weary of the study of
> real life. If they observed this duty conscientiously, they would give
> us fewer pictures chequered with vivid contrasts of light and shade;
> they would seldom elevate their heroes and heroines to the heights
> of rapture – still seldomer sink them to the depths of despair; for if
> we rarely taste the fulness of joy in this life, we yet more rarely
> savour the acid bitterness of hopeless anguish . . . .

It sounds as though the author is trying to persuade herself as much as
the reader. The statement is not only untrue, but was certainly wide
of Charlotte Brontë's own experience so soon after Brussels. Was she
trying to deny her own anguish, and its roots in sexual desire? The
passage which follows the above homily suggests that all blows can be
mitigated by courage and reason: it is a bleak philosophy, and the
exclusion of any mention of disappointed love is significant:

> But the man of regular life and rational mind never despairs. He
> loses his property – it is a blow – he staggers a moment; then, his
> energies, roused by the smart, are at work to seek a remedy;
> activity soon mitigates regret. Sickness affects him; he takes

patience – endures what he cannot cure . . .. Religion looks into
his desolate house with sunrise, and says, that in another world,
another life, he shall meet his kindred again.

Charlotte Brontë associated fire with sexual passion, and in her
novels key scenes between lovers tend to take place in front of the
hearth which, unlike the fire which burns down Rochester's house,
tends to be associated with regulated, properly controlled passion. In
Jane Eyre there is a key confrontation between Jane and Rochester,
when the latter dresses up as a fortune-teller and reads Jane's face by
the light of the fire: in *Shirley* Caroline sees the proud Shirley kneeling
at the fireside with her future husband, 'unconscious of the humility
of her present position'; and when Mrs Pryor chooses to be a
governess to escape a dreadful marriage she says: 'How safe seemed
the darkness and chill of an unkindled hearth, when no lurid
reflection from terror crimsoned its desolation!'[11]

The hearth also plays an important part in the coming together of
Crimsworth and Frances Henri, but the connotations are far from
fiery. Having found Frances in the Protestant cemetery, Crimsworth
walks her home. It starts to rain, and Frances invites him into her
modest, orderly little home. She has a green doormat on the
threshold, a fact which is mentioned several times, and green is a cool
colour, unlike red. The carpet in her living room is also green.
Crimsworth notices that there is no fire in the hearth, and Frances
insists on lighting one for his benefit. When he returns unexpectedly
she has already extinguished the fire. The reason given for her
behaviour is poverty, laudable parsimony. But the nature of Charlotte
Brontë's imagery taken overall makes it inevitable that we should
interpret this scene in a deeper way: Frances is sexually pure and
unawakened, but is capable of responding to him, and only him.
When Crimsworth leaves the house the rain has stopped and he sees a
rainbow, the nearest we ever get to the flaming skies of *Jane Eyre*.

Since the birth of psycho-analysis parsimony has been associated
with sexual suppression; they come naturally together in the
Protestant ethic, and the two themes become one in *The Professor*.

The male narrator allows Charlotte Brontë to distance herself from
the emotions of the heroine, with whom she would have identified too
closely for safety. But she is not at home inside Crimsworth. She had
a preference for strong, dominating heroes who manipulate women

but whilst, in the case of Rochester, that manipulation is forgiven because it is motivated by sexual passion, the denial of sexuality in *The Professor* makes Crimsworth appear sly, calculating and misogynistic. Whilst disapproving of his Roman Catholic pupils and their sexual depravity, he himself seems a rather nasty voyeur when he gets the boarded window of his bedroom opened up so that he can watch the girls in the garden below. Having suffered a setback in his advances to Zoraïde Reuter when he discovers that she is engaged, he goes out of his way to be nasty to her: 'her flatteries irritated my scorn'. As for Frances Henri, Crimsworth constantly emphasises that his attraction to her was not physical, that she was 'for a sensualist charmless, for me a treasure'. He admires her as the 'personification of discretion and forethought, of diligence and perseverance, of self-denial and self-control', someone for whom 'the more dangerous flame burned safely under the eye of reason'.[12] We are told that 'hopeless anguish' is reserved for those who 'have plunged like beasts into sensual indulgence'[13] whilst 'unlawful pleasure, trenching on another's rights, is delusive and envenomed pleasure – its hollowness disappoints at the time, its poison cruelly tortures afterwards, its effects deprave for ever'.[14] This comment comes rather unnecessarily from Crimsworth when he decides to leave his position as teacher on the eve of Mlle Reuter's marriage, and is clearly Brontë vindicating herself.

The Professor is a first novel which foreshadows many elements in Charlotte Brontë's later work. Frances Henri is clearly in the same mould as Jane Eyre and Lucy Snowe. The love relationship based on a master–pupil relationship between a young girl and an older man is here, and it was to recur in all her novels. Like Jane, Frances Henri calls her lover 'master', and there is more than a hint of Rochester in the way Crimsworth describes his bride as 'a curious mixture of tractability and firmness' and a 'vexing fairy'. But the differences between this and her later novels are more important. In all her books Charlotte Brontë would write of the pain and anguish of a woman in love; in *The Professor* she tried to deny the very existence of such emotions, precisely because she had been overwhelmed by them, and could not cope with the shame involved.

It is *Jane Eyre* which represents, at one level, a true wish-fulfilment fantasy, and by getting away from autobiography and realism and allowing her subconscious mind to dictate to her Charlotte Brontë made it possible to express her true wishes in fictional form. Rochester is a married man, but his wife is mad, hideous, an irrational wild beast who is quite unloved and ultimately dies, leaving Jane free to marry the man she never ceases to call 'my master', as Frances Henri greets Crimsworth in the churchyard: 'Mon maître!' Free of the inhibiting realism of the Brussels setting and transplanted to the world of Gothic romance, Charlotte is able to give her hero all the sexuality she deliberately denies William Crimsworth; indeed, Rochester has quite a record as a sexual libertine, and his very name suggests sexual licence.

The wish-fulfilment goes further. When Jane flees from Thornfield Hall, in misery and shame, much as Charlotte fled from Brussels, she finds refuge, not at Haworth, but at an idealised version of it. The two Rivers sisters, to whom the orphaned Jane Eyre finds herself related, are obviously based on Anne and Emily Brontë. When Charlotte returned to Haworth the family was in mourning for aunt Branwell, whilst the two Rivers sisters are wearing mourning for their father. Charlotte may not have wished to eliminate a somewhat tyrannical father-figure, but the transformation of Branwell into St John Rivers is certainly wish-fulfilment. Branwell's self-destructive urge, his restless ambition, is transformed into the missionary zeal of St John, which burns itself out in India, in a death which brings pride to the family, in contrast to Branwell's disintegration and death at home, which brought shame and disgrace on the family, particularly in Charlotte's eyes. Branwell succumbed to the seduction of rich Mrs Robinson, whilst St John coldly turns his back on the sexual attractions of the local young heiress. Even the family's old and gentlemanly lineage, in spite of present poverty, seems to reflect the fantasies of the Irish immigrant who changed his name from Patrick Brunty to Brontë. And the final wish-fulfilment with regard to the family comes when Jane Eyre inherits enough money to bring her 'sisters' home from their posts as governesses, something the three Brontë sisters always longed for – to be able to stay at home together under one roof.

However, this is only one layer of meaning in *Jane Eyre*. If it had been merely a romance of wish-fulfilment it would not have had the power which both attracted and repelled contemporary readers. *Jane Eyre* deals forcefully and explicitly with the central contradictions of a woman's life just tactfully hinted at in *Deerbrook*; but it does more than that, it expresses the contradiction involved in seeking love from the very object one has cause to hate and fear as the oppressor. Anger and rebellion is as much a motivating force in the novel as sexual passion.

The childhood of Jane Eyre encapsulates the traumatic transformation which society imposes on the girl-child to turn her into an acceptable adult woman. Her rebellion in the Reed household is sparked off by the fact that young John Reed, conscious of his position as the male son and heir, insists that Jane should call him 'Master Reed'. Verbal abuse is followed by physical force, and she is conscious of the fact that she 'had no appeal whatever against either his menaces or his inflictions', even while she finds the boy physically repulsive. John Reed lectures her on the facts of life: 'Now, I'll teach you to rummage my book-shelves: for they *are* mine; all the house belongs to me, or will do in a few years.' After which he quite literally 'throws the book at her', knocking her down. Jane's terror is quickly succeeded by anger: ' . . . you are like a slave-driver – you are like the Roman emperors!' she shouts at him.[15] She is relegated to the care of the servants, and when one of them chides her for striking 'your young master' she retorts hotly: 'How is he my master? Am I a servant?'[16] Young Jane at Gateshead resents being relegated to the level of servant, just as the governess at Thornfield would do.

But her punishment for rebelling against the young master is to be locked in the red room, an incident which is clearly a form of symbolic sexual initiation, frightening and punitive. As we have already seen, from its association with fire the colour red always had sexual connotations for Charlotte Brontë. The room has an awesome, terrifying sanctity, because it contains the huge empty bed with crimson hangings in which Mr Reed, the true master of the house, died. The room is the hidden, crimson inner space of woman's sexuality, one could almost call it Mrs Reed's vagina. We are told that this sanctuary is 'lonely in spite of its grandeur', that since the death of Mr Reed 'a sense of dreary consecration had guarded it from frequent intrusion', and that Mrs Reed occasionally visited the room 'to review the contents of a certain secret drawer', which sounds distinctly masturbatory.[17]

Now it is Jane's turn to become a woman, to have the tomboy knocked out of her and to go through the fearful initiation involved in becoming an acceptable woman. 'I was conscious that a moment's mutiny had already rendered me liable to strange penalties.' In a male-dominated society sexual initiation is punitive. She must become passive and allow terrifying things to be done to her. In the red room Jane only promises to sit still when the servants prepare to tie her down: 'If you don't sit still, you must be tied down.' Locked in the red room, Jane thinks about her inability to please, and thinks with jealousy of cousin Georgiana's beauty, which purchased 'indemnity for every fault'. She also broods on the 'young master' John Reed, somebody:

> no one thwarted, much less punished; though he twisted the necks of the pigeons, killed the little pea-chicks, set the dogs at the sheep, stripped the hothouse of their fruit, and broke the buds of the choicest plants in the conservatory: he called his mother 'old girl,' too; sometimes reviled her for her dark skin, similar to his own; bluntly disregarded her wishes; not unfrequently tore and spoiled her silk attire; and he was still 'her own darling'.

As the male son and heir John Reed is given total licence to give vent to his aggressive and destructive instincts, something which will later bring ruin on the entire family. But at another level this description, like the scene between John and Jane in the first chapter when the boy throws a book at her, is a parody of the marital relationship. John Reed can treat his mother as he will later treat a wife.

Locked up in the red room, Jane thinks about 'escape from insupportable oppression – as running away, or if that could not be effected, neither eating or drinking more, and letting myself die' – that is, the anorexia nervosa of female adolescence. Having persuaded herself that the ghost of Mr Reed is in the red room she panics, pleads to be allowed to remain a child: 'Take me out! Let me go to the nursery!' but her cries do not get the desired response. On the contrary, the servants disapprove of her screaming: 'If she had been in great pain one would have excused it' is the comment, again suggesting sexual initiation. And this interpretation is reinforced when Mrs Reed comes to the room and tells her: 'You will now stay here an hour longer, and it is only on condition of perfect submission and stillness that I shall liberate you then.' Terrified of the ghost of Mr Reed, though she also feels that if he were alive 'he would have treated me kindly', Jane faints. This is the point of physical submission, and when she returns to consciousness she is 'aware that some one was handling me; lifting me up and supporting me in a sitting posture, and that more tenderly than I had ever been raised or upheld before'. She has become the delicate female sexual object, to be petted and pandered in return for submission and passivity. Jane's illness after the incarceration in the red room is paralleled in *Wuthering Heights* by the way the tomboy Catherine Earnshaw is nursed at Thrushcross Grange and returns to Wuthering Heights as a fine young lady dressed in fancy clothes, who will not play with Heathcliff because he is scruffy.

The narrator of *Jane Eyre* is Jane herself ten years after she has become Mrs Rochester. Of the incident in the red room the narrator comments: 'No severe or prolonged bodily illness followed this incident of the red-room: it only gave my nerves a shock, of which I feel the reverberation to this day.'[18] And as though to underline the fact that sexual initiation involves the death of freedom of the spirit for a woman, the end of the wild thing, the tomboy, the servant Bessie sings a song at her beside which begins: 'In the days when we went gipsying/A long time ago . . .' and young Jane responds to the song with the comment: 'I had often heard the song before, and always with lively delight; . . . . But now . . . I found in its melody an indescribable sadness . . . ''A long time ago'' came out like the saddest cadence of a funeral hymn.'

The incident in the red room is only the beginning of the process designed to break the rebellious spirit of Jane, who is 'a heterogeneous thing . . . a noxious thing, cherishing the germs of indignation at their treatment'.[19] The symbolic sexual initiation or rape is followed by her 'schooling' at Lowood, which in Freudian terms is the castration phase. But before Jane is sent to Lowood there is a very significant conversation with the apothecary, who visits the sick Jane after she has been shut up in the red room. When he asks her: 'Are you not thankful to have such a fine place to live at?' Jane replies: 'It is not my house, sir; and Abbot says I have less right to be here than a servant.'[20] Once more the house as patriarchal domain is a central image, but Jane Eyre gives a very different response to the grateful acceptance of Fanny Price in *Mansfield Park*. The apothecary asks the child whether she would mind living with poor people, but the narrator comments: 'I was not heroic enough to purchase liberty at the price of caste.' This was the essential difference between Charlotte and Emily Brontë: Charlotte resented the social down-grading which poor women of good family had to suffer, and her heroine resents being treated like a servant. Emily, on the other hand, did not care about class distinctions, was at home in the kitchen, and purchased true freedom of spirit as a woman. In

Wuthering Heights her heroine is condemned to death precisely because she does forfeit her liberty to become part of the caste system. Charlotte loved and admired Emily, and at this point in the narrative she seems dimly aware of a radical alternative which neither she nor her heroine, for all her spirit, is quite heroic enough to take. Almost apologetically she comments: 'Poverty looks grim to grown people; still more so to children . . . they think of the word only as connected with ragged clothes, scanty food, fireless grates, rude manners, and debasing vices: poverty for me was synonymous with degradation.' The images here listed were certainly not synonymous with degradation for Emily: on the contrary.

Lowood School is a charity institution run by the Church, and Charlotte Brontë puts strong emphasis on the way the patriarchal church teaches women to bite the dust. When Mr Brocklehurst arrives at Gateshead to collect Jane he says: 'No sight so sad as that of a naughty child . . . especially a naughty little girl'[21] and when Mrs Reed says she wants Jane 'to be made useful, to be kept humble' he assures her 'I have studied how best to mortify in them the worldly sentiment of pride.' Male Christianity and its degradation of women is contrasted with true Christianity in the shape of Miss Temple (again the name is significant), but as a woman she is devoid of power, and 'has to answer to Mr Brocklehurst for all she does'. Young Jane reads the text on the school wall and finds it highly ambiguous: 'Let your light so shine before men that they may see your good works, and glorify your Father which is in heaven'. Should women shine 'before men' and the male God in heaven? 'I read these words over and over again: I felt that an explanation belonged to them, and was unable fully to penetrate their import.'[22]

Mortification of the flesh amounting to sexual castration is the schooling given to girls at Lowood. Going to church is associated with discomfort and frigidity: 'We set out cold, we arrived at church colder: during the morning service we became almost paralysed.'[23] Only Helen Burns (note the surname) is immune to the harsh treatment. She retreats into daydreams, and literally burns up inside. She dies whilst lying in the same bed with Jane, as though she was her *alter ego*. Only after her marriage to Rochester is this libidinous *alter ego* resurrected, when Mrs Rochester puts a tombstone on her grave with the one word RESURGAM.

Sexual repression in women at puberty involves castration, the 'abandonment' of clitoral sexuality which, as Freud put it, involves a 'wave of repression at puberty, which as it were, puts aside their childish masculinity' and accounts for woman's greater proneness to neurosis and hysteria.[24] Mr Brocklehurst, 'standing on the hearth' (of course!) surveys the girls and is appalled to see a girl with red curls. Miss Temple explains that the girl's hair curls naturally, whereupon he exclaims: 'Naturally! Yes, but we are not to conform to nature: I wish these girls to be the children of Grace.' He then orders all the girls to stand facing the wall, inspects them, and orders: 'All these top-knots must be cut off.' When Miss Temple tries to remonstrate she is told: 'I have a Master to serve whose kingdom is not of this world: my mission is to mortify in these girls the lusts of the flesh.'[25]

After the death of Helen Burns, and under the tutelage of Miss Temple, Jane seems a reformed character. The day-dreaming Helen, her *alter ego* and libido, had told Jane: 'By dying young, I shall escape great sufferings. I had not qualities or talents to make my way well in the world: I should have been continually at fault.'[26] The Jane who was left behind appears, in time, to be properly schooled: 'I had given allegiance to duty and order: I was quiet; I believed I was content: to the eyes of others, usually even to my own, I appeared a disciplined and subdued character.'[27] But Miss Temple, with her feminine version of Christianity leaves Lowood to get married, and Jane becomes restless: 'I was left in my natural element, and beginning to feel the stirrings of old emotions.' This restlessness takes her straight to Thornfield Hall (again the name is significant) a field of thorns which seems to promise 'flowers and pleasures, as well as thorns and toils'.[28]

Having been brought low at Lowood, and now entering upon the thorny field of sexuality, Jane begins to think about her appearance, dresses herself with as much care as her few clothes will permit and becomes conscious of her want of beauty. The main drawing room, decorated in red and white in 'a general blending of snow and fire' seems to Jane 'a glimpse of a fairy place, so bright to my novice eyes'. Snow and fire, hot and cold, red and white are the constant, familiar polarities of Charlotte Brontë's sexual imagery. Unlike Rochester Jane is a novice to sex but Jane Air, his Ariel, the woman he constantly refers to as his elf, spirit, fairy, belongs to this 'fairy place'.

But there is a problem, in the shape of the first Mrs Rochester, who not only provides the obvious impediment but also represents a dreadful warning: she embodies all Jane's fears about marriage within a male-dominated society. Mrs Rochester has gone mad, is imprisoned on the third storey of the house, and if Jane agrees to marry she will herself become a prisoner, a prey to rage and frustration. When Jane is overcome by a feeling of frustration at her woman's destiny, when she longs to get out into the larger world, she goes to the roof of the house to give vent to these feelings, and when the crazed Mrs Rochester sets fire to the house she escapes to the roof before jumping to her death. Just as the imprisoned Mrs Rochester paces up and down on the third floor, so Jane also paces:

> . . . the restlessness was in my nature; it agitated me to pain sometimes. Then my sole relief was to walk along the corridor of the third story, backwards and forwards, safe in the silence and solitude of the spot . . . .[29]

We have already seen how Mary Wollstonecraft used the Gothic novel of female imprisonment to express the wrongs of woman, but it was Charlotte Brontë who gave female Gothic narrative its ultimate force and meaning. She did it naturally, probably only half knowing what she was at, which is why the whole story has the compelling quality of myth.

When Jane first sees the third storey at Thornfield Hall she is reminded of Bluebeard's castle, and the story has obvious parallels with that of Bluebeard. Men destroy their wives, both because of the nature of their sexuality and because of their economic advantages, and both problems have to be solved before Jane can become Rochester's wife. Only by making Rochester a tired, hopeless cripple who will stray no more and Jane a woman with an independent income can the author unite her heroine with the man she loves. We have an augury of the need to cut the hero down to size at their very first meeting, when Rochester falls off his horse and is very reluctant to take the assistance Jane offers. It is a neat, probably subconscious reversal of the situation in those earlier women's novels where a heroine is rescued from a runaway horse by the hero.

Named after the Earl of Rochester, the hero represents sexuality rather than romantic love or suitable marriage. He is a libertine, has travelled widely and kept mistresses. Jane first meets him in the red and white drawing room, 'basking in the light and heat of a superb fire', and a few pages further on he is again standing in front of the fireplace 'with so much unconscious pride in his port', while 'the large fire was all red and clear'. Rochester first has to undo the sexual repression of her education, and he tells her so:

> The Lowood constraint still clings to you somewhat; controlling your features, muffling your voice and restricting your limbs; and you fear in the presence of a man . . . to smile too gaily, speak too freely, or move too quickly: but in time, I think you will learn to be natural with me . . . .[30]

Jane quickly recognises that Rochester is a typical dominant male, 'harsh to inferiority of every description', and that 'his great kindness to me was balanced by unjust severity to many others'.[31] But she needs him; when she lies awake at night thinking of him she hears Mrs Rochester's demoniac laughter, something which seems to come from within herself: 'I thought at first the goblin-laughter stood at my bed-side – or rather, crouched at my pillow'. Immediately afterwards she finds the curtains of Rochester's bed on fire. Fire, we know, had strong sexual associations for Charlotte Brontë and in Bertha Rochester, sexually spurned, it runs out of control and becomes dangerous. It is the weapon she uses twice, on the second occasion burning down the house and blinding Rochester. But on the first occasion, when Jane lies awake thinking of Rochester and hears the wild laughter coming, it seems, from her own pillow, fire also represents animal sexuality unhallowed by matrimony (fire within the hearth) which has to be put down. Jane puts out the fire round Rochester's bed, and the terms used by the author are significant:

> I . . . deluged the bed and its occupant, flew back to my own room, brought my own water-jug, baptized the couch afresh, and, by God's aid, succeeded in extinguishing the flames which were devouring it.[32]

Conscious Christian piety helps to suppress the unruly libido. But there is also a suggestion that Jane Eyre, the elf, sprite, good fairy, with her rather priggish morality, will ultimately reform Rochester the libertine. Rochester seems to recognise that a two-way process of change is taking place when he wakes with the words: 'In the names of all the elves in Christendom, is that Jane Eyre? . . . What have you done with me, witch, sorceress?'

Flattered by Rochester's attentions, Jane begins to have dreams of upward mobility through marriage. She wonders whether the servant Grace Poole had once been Rochester's mistress:

> I hastened to drive from my mind the hateful notion I had been conceiving respecting Grace Poole; it disgusted me. I compared myself with her, and found we were different. Bessie Leaven [*the first time this curious surname appears!*] had said I was quite the lady; and she spoke truth: I was a lady.[33]

But when Rochester plays on her emotions by paying court to Blanche Ingram, Jane is brought rudely back to earth and a true assessment of her situation as an 'indigent and insignificant plebian'. She tells herself 'He is not of your order; keep to your caste' and broods on the dangerous fire of secret love. But Rochester knows all about the secret fire which is consuming Jane. When he pretends to be a fortune teller and reads Jane's face in the light of the library fire he tells her: 'You are cold, because you are alone: no contact strikes the fire from you that is in you.' He stirs the actual fire so he can see her better as she kneels on the hearth, and the bemused Jane, who seems very obtuse in not recognising Rochester, finally tells him: 'Don't keep me long; the fire scorches me.'[34]

Bertha Rochester is an impediment to marriage because she embodies an awful warning, both Jane's and the author's anxieties about what marriage does to women. The mood changes when Jane agrees to marry Rochester. Instead of being deliriously happy, Jane becomes tense and unhappy: she resents the way Rochester treats her, the way he buys clothes for her as though she were a doll; she wants to continue to earn her keep as Adèle's governess, and resents being called an 'angel'. She tells him that, like all men, he will tire of her in six months and that when his ardour cools 'I shall have much ado to please you', and the thought of changing her name to Rochester fills her with 'something that smote and stunned: it was, I think, almost fear.'[35] It is her sense of annoyance and degradation at being a kept woman which leads her to write to her uncle in Madeira, which in turn exposes the bigamy.

The reader is left in no doubt of the fact that Jane Eyre is dreading her wedding day. 'There was no putting off the day that advanced – the bridal day . . . .' She cannot bear to label her bridal luggage with her new name because it means a loss of identity. Just as she shared a bed with her dying *alter ego*, Helen Burns, during the earlier *rite de passage* involved in becoming an acceptable woman, she shares a bed with little Adèle the night before the wedding, as protection from the mad imprisoned spirit on the third storey, who has torn her wedding veil, the fancy veil which Rochester had given her and which Jane herself would have liked to destroy:

> With little Adèle in my arms, I watched the slumber of childhood – so tranquil, so passionless, so innocent . . . . I remember Adèle clung to me as I left her . . . and I cried over her as I loosened her little hands from my neck . . . . She seemed the semblance of my past life; and he, I was now to array myself to meet, the dread, but adored, type of my unknown future day.[36]

Because the madwoman has destroyed the fancy veil Jane has to wear the simple one she herself chose, and later that day she comes face to face with the first Mrs Rochester, running backwards and forwards in a room without a window, where a fire burns, 'guarded by a high and strong fender'. Jane is now face to face with her own future. She reproaches Rochester for his callous disregard:

> 'You speak of her with hate – with vindictive antipathy. It is cruel – she cannot help being mad.'
> ' . . . it is not because she is mad I hate her. If you were mad, do you think I should hate you?'
> 'I do indeed, sir.'[37]

Sexual temptation is strong, but self-preservation is stronger. Jane has heard him speak of his foreign mistresses, and knows he would one day regard her with the same contempt. She dreams of the red room, hears a voice say 'My daughter, flee temptation' and leaves Thornfield Hall.

Jane finds refuge and a humble independence with the Rivers family, but St John Rivers as a suitor is unsatisfactory because he is at the other extreme from Rochester, and would deny her natural sexuality completely. She cannot face marriage with him:

> forced to keep the fire of my nature continually low, to compel it to burn inwardly and never utter a cry, though the imprisoned flame consumed vital after vital – *this* would be unendurable.[38]

Like Brocklehurst at Lowood, St John represents an unacceptable male Christianity which tries to deny women their natural sexuality. When Jane tells St John that his coldness and lack of love would kill her he reproves her in words that reveal his disgust with female sexuality: 'Your words are such as ought not to be used: violent, unfeminine, and untrue.' Though Rochester and St John are poles apart they do have certain things in common: both of them try to dominate Jane with their masculine will, but the 'freezing' servitude St John has to offer drives her back to Rochester, safe in the knowledge that she now has money of her own, which makes her independent. And Rochester's days of roving sexuality are over: when the ostler at the inn tells Jane that he is blind and a cripple, he adds with what sounds suspiciously like satisfaction: 'he can't get out of England, I fancy – he's a fixture now.'[39] The roles are very obviously reversed, with Jane in control, teasing him, and taking considerable delight in rousing his sexual jealousy. Only after Rochester has learned to acknowledge his dependence on Jane is he allowed by the author to become less helpless through a partial recovery of his sight.

Charlotte Brontë was herself a victim of the conflicts which beset a woman born into the Victorian age. In *Jane Eyre*, by allowing her subconscious to take over she created a powerful myth which embodied the socio-sexual conflicts which any thinking, feeling woman was heir to. When G. H. Lewes warned her against melodrama she answered:

> imagination is a strong, restless faculty, which claims to be heard and exercised; are we to be quite deaf to her cry, and insensate to her struggles?[40]

The 'imagination' she speaks of is visualised in terms of an imprisoned woman, crying to be heard, struggling to gain her freedom. In *Jane Eyre*, by allowing her subconscious to take command, and subdue the subduing superego of the prim and self-conscious vicar's daughter, she permitted the cry of the suppressed inner woman to be heard in terms which have had an immediate appeal to generations of women readers. Contemporary readers who were shocked by the book were rightly shocked. As Mrs Rigby wrote in the *Quarterly Review* in 1848:

the tone of mind and thought which has overthrown authority and violated every code human and divine abroad, and fostered Chartism and rebellion at home is the same which has also written *Jane Eyre*.

If Charlotte Brontë was distressed by such comments it was because her conscious mind refused to accept, fully, what her subconscious mind, or 'imagination', was doing. But the inner woman in her was seething with the spirit of rebellion.

8. Wuthering Heights

JANE Austen achieved greatness as a woman writer in a man's world by making herself small, by staying quietly in her corner of the drawing room and behaving with all the decorum expected of her sex. Emily Brontë achieved greatness as a woman writer by making herself tall, by simply rising above the social conflict between the sexes and ignoring it. Austen's behaviour may have been a cunning stratagem, but Emily Brontë was a free spirit: she ignored the constraints placed on women because for her they did not exist, and therefore did not impinge upon her consciousness.

Unlike Charlotte, Emily felt no resentment or frustration at having been born a woman. She did household chores as naturally and with as little fuss as she did everything else. Baking bread was as much a part of life as playing the piano or walking on the moors. Far from longing for wider horizons, as Charlotte did, Emily was only happy at Haworth and on her beloved moors. Charlotte felt that her sex made her an inadequate writer, and her letters are full of a sense of inferiority to Dickens and Thackeray, because their writing reflects a broader knowledge of the scenes of the busy world. Emily had no such feeling of inadequacy: her home ground gave her a cosmic vision of man in his fundamental setting, nature, which was more than enough to feed her literary imagination. She was never, like Charlotte, plagued by the illusion that the world beyond the horizon was more important and more meaningful because it was out of reach. As for the great literary world, which Charlotte entered with shy trepidation, Emily simply had no time for it. She had a sure eye and ear for everything that was false and untrue in poetry, and this made her immune to praise and blame alike. Charlotte Brontë makes this clear in her portrait of Shirley, modelled on Emily:

> Few, Shirley conceived, men or women have the right taste in poetry: the right sense for discriminating between what is real and what is false. She had again and again heard very clever people pronounce this or that passage, in this or that versifier, altogether

admirable, which, when she read, her soul refused to acknowledge as anything but cant, flourish, and tinsel, or at best, elaborate wordiness . . .[1]

In Brussels, M. Heger thought that Emily ought to have been born a man, in which case she might have become a navigator. He was impressed by her will, and her lack of physical fear was obvious to all. Indeed, it became almost legendary. She was also a very self-contained person, who spoke very little, wrote no letters, and kept her thoughts to herself. And she seems to have been emotionally immune to the opposite sex.

If Emily kept her thoughts to herself, it was partly because they would have been regarded as unconventional and shocking, particularly her ideas on religion. Her father was broadminded enough to excuse Emily from regular church attendance, and she did not take Sunday school classes, even when her sisters were away and there was a shortage of teachers. We are told that she would never be drawn on the subject of organised religion. Hardly surprising, since her outlook was essentially pagan, and her writing shows a vision of man as part of a great natural cycle, in which all must return to earth, but where the strong survive a little longer than the weak. She already understood what Charles Darwin discovered, and his *Origin of Species* would not have surprised or shocked her. Charlotte's lifelong friend, Ellen Nussey, recalled Emily out walking on the moors at the age of fifteen: 'Emily, half reclining on a slab of stone, played like a young child with the tadpoles in the water, making them swim about, and then fell to moralizing on the strong and the weak, the brave and the cowardly, as she chased them with her hand.'[2]

Charlotte must have had some inkling of these ideas of Emily's. In *Shirley* the heroine is referred to as a 'pagan'. It in part explains the apologetic embarrassment that Charlotte evinced about her dead sister's work, and perhaps explains the fact that no unfinished manuscript survived Emily's death. Although religion was to some extent a torment to Charlotte, it was also a shield against the world, and she was just as anxious to protect her sister as herself.

Although there are certain surface similarities between the childhood conflicts of Jane Eyre and of Catherine Earnshaw in *Wuthering Heights*, qualitatively they are on an entirely different level. Charlotte's heroine is essentially a rebellious victim of a society which oppresses women, whereas Catherine, although she is female, is seen essentially as an individual with freedom of choice: she makes the wrong choice and is punished. She herself recognises the justice of her doom. Catherine Earnshaw is a very rare phenomenon in nineteenth-century fiction: a heroine who dies through inner moral necessity, and is not destroyed by the author because she has broken the social taboos against women.

The action of *Wuthering Heights* takes place against a background of nature which is an essential element in the story, which has cosmic as well as human dimensions which makes it in many ways comparable to *King Lear*, to which it bears some resemblance. Certainly the arguments about the nature of nature, which are explicit in *King Lear*, are implicit in the novel, where the conflict of values is between nature and civilisation, the two polarities being represented by the two houses and their inhabitants, Wuthering Heights representing nature and Thrushcross Grange civilisation. Catherine Earnshaw's *alter ego* is neither a madwoman imprisoned by man nor a girl who dies at puberty, but Heathcliff, a man who is more herself than she is, as she herself is the first to admit. We do not know whether Emily Brontë believed the sexes to be essentially androgynous, though we do know that her own behaviour was often 'mannish'. Perhaps she thought that for women to be true to themselves, more 'natural', they should behave more like men. There is an interesting clue to her sister's possible attitude in her portrait of Emily in *Shirley*. Caroline asks Shirley whether men are superior to women, whereupon the latter answers: 'I would scorn to contend for empire with him . . . . Shall my left hand dispute for precedence with my right? – Shall my heart quarrel with my pulse?'[3]

Whatever her opinions, Emily Brontë rose above the war of the sexes by taking a much broader view. Free herself, she placed her characters against a cosmic background in which they were themselves free to play out their destinies, and it is this grandeur and simplicity of vision which gives her novel its enduring force and makes it a unique achievement, comparable only to Shakespeare, both in its poetic scope and its powerful use of language.

Emily Brontë's theme concerns nature and civilisation, and her use of languages plays an integral part in the development of this theme. The first person narrative technique is, as many people have noted, a very complex and apparently convoluted affair, but it serves a very specific purpose. Far from being a subjective first person narrative, as in *Jane Eyre* (a narrative which is often turgid), the first person narration in *Wuthering Heights*, taken over like a stick in a relay race, makes both for a sense of immediacy and a directness and objectivity which no mere authorial voice could have achieved. But there is more to it than that: in the struggle between nature and civilisation Nelly Dean represents a kind of norm; she is the only person who moves naturally between the two warring houses and her way of speaking represents an acceptable norm, natural and forthright, which makes it right for her to be the principal storyteller. Remember that the narrative is begun by Lockwood, civilised gentleman from the south (and north and south are also related polarities in the novel). Lockwood's language is soon held up to ridicule, one almost feels that he represents the typical voice of the upper-class novels which were fashionable at the time, and which Emily Brontë begins by parodying and ends by rejecting. Heathcliff sneers at Lockwood for calling Catherine Heathcliff 'your amiable lady', which is both florid cant and totally inappropriate. Having established that Lockwood is totally unequipped to tell this story, any story, because his civilised background has estranged him from both nature and human nature, Emily drops him and allows Nelly Dean to take over. Her language is direct and simple, not florid, like Lockwood's, nor crude and incomprehensible like Joseph's. She represents a sensible norm between nature and culture, is employed by both Heathcliff and Edgar Linton in turn, and although she is a poor man's daughter has read all the books at Thrushcross Grange, except Latin and Greek.

Language is always an important indicator in the novel. People from different layers of society – and the polished upper classes are usually invaders from the south, as opposed to the rude indigenous population – often fail to understand each other. When the child Heathcliff first arrives in the Earnshaw household he speaks a gibberish which nobody can understand. When the younger Catherine from the Grange first meets her cousin Hareton it is his rude language which shocks her. That he should swear at her, 'she who was always "love," and "darling," and "queen," and "angel," with everybody at the Grange, to be insulted so shockingly by a stranger! She did not comprehend it.'[4] Now, although Hareton undoubtedly needs civilising, and Catherine ultimately succeeds in making him both literate and less uncouth, it is also true that words like 'queen' and 'angel' are ludicrous falsehoods when applied to a young woman, represent the lies which nineteenth-century civilisation told about women. Hareton may need to become more civilised, but young Catherine Linton needs to come in contact with a more natural world.

The fact that Emily Brontë rose above the war between the sexes does not mean she totally ignored its implications, simply that she incorporated these factors into a more total vision of humanity. Both Emily and Charlotte Brontë see their heroines as naturally wild and rebellious in childhood, before undergoing a fundamental change in adolescence. Catherine loses her father and comes under the tyrannical rule of her brother, just as Jane Eyre loses father and uncle and is bullied by John Reed. 'I wish my father were back again. Hindley is a detestable substitute' she writes in the book which Lockwood discovers, and Hindley's words 'You forget you have a master here'[5] echo those of John Reed. Catherine, like Jane, detests the gloomy piety of Sundays; Jane hides in the window seat behind the curtains, Catherine and Heathcliff try to create their own world by hiding in the arch under the dresser, pinning their pinafores together as a curtain. The patriarchal master of the house in *Wuthering Heights* punishes Catherine through her natural *alter ego*, Heathcliff, who is banished to the servants' quarters as Jane, at Gateshead, is also banished to the servants' quarters after her act of rebellion.

But the crucial turning point, the *rite de passage* between girlhood and womanhood, is quite different. Catherine Earnshaw, accompanied by Heathcliff, trespasses on the grounds of Thrushcross Grange, and is bitten by a dog. The Lintons take her in, drive away Heathcliff, her 'natural' *alter ego*, and make an unnatural, pampered lady of her. Heathcliff and Catherine, while dazzled by the finery of the Grange, had despised the behaviour of the pampered, spoiled Linton children; now it is Catherine's turn to be laid up on a sofa, that symbol of the Victorian emasculation of women, the constant invalidism which went with being a civilised lady. Tomboy Catherine is transformed, dressed up in fine clothes, her hair curled, while Heathcliff vainly tries to gain access to her. But the essential point is that nobody forces Catherine to undergo a change as Jane is forced: she herself is seduced by the finery and chooses to become different. She is fully aware that she is doing wrong in denying her nature, and that she is doing it to escape the poverty and humiliation of the disinherited daughter of the house. She tells Nelly: 'I've no more business to marry Edgar Linton than I have to be in heaven; and if the wicked man in there [i.e. Hindley] had not brought Heathcliff so low, I shouldn't have thought of it.'[6] This after she dreamt she was in heaven, which 'did not seem to be my home', and she wept for joy to find herself back at the Heights. Heathcliff, being her natural self, is indeed more herself than she is, and the moment she decides not to marry him he disappears, bringing on a severe illness from which she never fully recovers.

Like young Jane Eyre, Catherine Earnshaw has chosen caste instead of liberty, but in *Wuthering Heights* this is the central, existential choice, on which everything else depends, whilst in *Jane Eyre* no clear alternative is envisaged, only compromise. Liberty means being oneself, and Catherine has turned her back on the natural, masculine side of herself. She is a changed woman after her illness and Heathcliff's disappearance, and the doctor warns that her mental and physical health are precarious. The happiness of Catherine and Edgar is false and short-lived, and Nelly comments: 'Well, we *must* be for ourselves in the long run; the mild and generous are only more justly selfish than the domineering . . . .'[7]

The happiness of the couple ends with the return of Heathcliff who, being her natural self, keeps intruding at the Grange. The doctor had warned that Catherine must not be 'crossed' at any price, but Edgar does cross Catherine by trying to exclude Heathcliff. Not being a gentleman, and civilised, Linton insists he should come no further than the kitchen, where Catherine mockingly proposes to join him, if she is not enough of a 'lady' for him. Edgar forbids Heathcliff to come to the Grange at all; violent scenes, so much a part of everyday life at the Heights, are narrowly avoided at the Grange, but at enormous psychological cost. Catherine rightly feels that the tussle between these two men, the two opposing forces of nature and civilisation, is tearing her apart and destroying her. Heathcliff, representing natural forces, is also right when he says that if he were in Linton's position he would not have behaved in the same way, excluding her true nature, and the man she cares for.

Catherine tries to achieve upward mobility through marriage. Significantly, she justifies her marriage to Linton by telling Nelly that through this marriage she will be able to help Heathcliff, her real self, to rise in the world, and that 'if I marry Linton, I can aid Heathcliff to rise, and place him out of my brother's power'. But Nelly warns her that she is nursing a dangerous delusion if she thinks marriage will give freedom to her true self: 'You'll find him not so pliable as you calculate upon: and though I'm hardly a judge, I think that's the worst motive you've given yet for being the wife of young Linton.'[8] Many women deluded themselves into believing that marriage could provide an escape from domestic male tyranny, and many women writers had warned against marriage for this reason. It is Emily's genius to lift this theme on to a higher plane and turn it into a great myth involving basic values. Ironically Heathcliff has no need to be 'helped': being a natural force he takes what he wants and finds no difficulty in becoming rich and self-sufficient.

Isabella Linton follows the opposite path from Catherine, and moves from the civilised life of the Grange to Wuthering Heights. Once there she becomes 'a thorough little slattern', makes no attempt to maintain civilised standards of behaviour and, like the other inmates of the Heights, makes no attempt to control her natural passions. Once her delusive infatuation for Heathcliff turns to hatred she becomes just as wild and bloodthirsty as anyone else at the Heights, and thinks seriously of helping to kill Heathcliff. Edgar Linton, who is indeed far from 'pliable', is rigid in not forgiving his sister for her lapse from civilised standards, and Isabella disappears to the civilised south, where she gives birth to a lily-livered son who is the embodiment of civilisation brought to the point of degeneracy.

The banishment of Heathcliff from Thrushcross Grange brings on a return of Catherine's illness, and this time it is mortal. All along we are made aware that it is her will that is involved, that 'we must be for ourselves in the long run', because that is the way of nature; Nelly feels that Catherine is wilfully making herself ill, by not eating, for instance, and the doctor's warning that she must not be 'crossed' is remembered when it is already too late. Civilised Edgar stays aloof too long, and when Heathcliff finally forces an entry he insists that she alone is to blame for her fate:

> *Why* did you despise me? *Why* did you betray your own heart, Cathy? I have not one word of comfort. You deserve this. You have killed yourself . . . . Because misery, and degradation, and death, and nothing that God or satan could inflict would have parted us, *you*, of your own will, did it. I have not broken your heart – you have broken it . . . .[9]

And Catherine acknowledges the truth of his words: 'If I've done wrong, I'm dying for it.' But she always did know. At Wuthering Heights, where she behaved more naturally, more like her true self, she told Nelly that she was unhappy about turning her back on Heathcliff and marrying Edgar: 'In my soul and in my heart, I'm convinced I'm wrong!'

Even while the couple are apparently happy, Catherine is subject to fits of depression, which Edgar does not understand, and which are attributed to her illness after Heathcliff's sudden disappearance. When Heathcliff returns Catherine tells Nelly that she has suffered bitter misery in his absence, and that she hid her unhappiness from Edgar. Sex as an element in the normal relationship between man and woman in marriage is an irrelevance in this narrative, as it is irrelevant between Heathcliff and Catherine. Catherine, by marrying Edgar, has separated herself from her true self, Heathcliff, an unnatural act which must have dire consequences, and Edgar, because of the sort of man he is, will not allow her to be herself. Catherine has no illusions about Heathcliff, since he is herself, and she knows herself to be fierce, wilful, and capable of cruelty, and she tries to warn the 'infantile' Isabella, whom Nelly describes as 'possessed of keen wit, keen feelings, and a keen temper' that she is deluding herself. Ambition, said Nelly, had led Catherine 'to adopt a double character without exactly intending to deceive any one. In the place where she had heard Heathcliff termed a "vulgar young ruffian," and "worse than a brute," she took care not to act like him; but at home she had small inclination to practise politeness that would only be laughed at, and restrain an unruly nature when it would bring her neither credit nor praise.'[10] Before her marriage Catherine tries to play the lady with Linton and be herself with Heathcliff, but this double character, this duplicity makes it necessary to keep the two men apart: 'for when Heathcliff expressed contempt of Linton in his presence, she could not half coincide, as she did in his absence; and when Linton evinced disgust and antipathy to Heathcliff, she dared not treat his sentiments with indifference, as if depreciation of her playmate were of scarcely any consequence to her'. Heathcliff is her playmate, her companion from early childhood, her natural tomboy self, to be spurned for the sake of civilised marriage and all it entails.

It is significant that when Catherine is dying she does not think and dream of Heathcliff, but of her own childhood at the Heights. To make Nelly understand the nature of her inner torment, she tells her:

. . . supposing at twelve years old, I had been wrenched from the Heights, and every early association, and my all in all, as

Heathcliff was at that time, and been converted at a stroke into Mrs Linton, the lady of Thrushcross Grange, and the wife of a stranger: an exile, and outcast, thenceforth, from what had been my world – You may fancy a glimpse of the abyss where I grovelled.[11]

Her sick nightmare encapsulates the truth, and it is significant that Catherine puts the transformation as happening at the age of twelve, not the date of her marriage, but the time of that first visit to the Grange, the painful *rite de passage* of adolescence with its alienation from the true self. And if there is any doubt left of the nature of Catherine's loss, which is a loss of self and not of a love object, she goes on: 'I wish I were a girl again, half savage, and hardy, and free . . .. Why am I so changed?'

Heathcliff, representing nature, like the natural son Edmund in *King Lear*, takes revenge on the legitimate who inherit and succeed by excluding him, leaving him out of account. Heathcliff and Edgar are opposing forces as Edmund and Edgar are in *Lear*, and those who represent legitimacy and ordered civilisation and try to ignore the force of nature bring retribution on themselves. Lear and Gloucester are punished as Edgar and Hindley are punished, but whilst Shakespeare makes Cordelia an image of innocence and truth, and a victim, Emily Brontë made her female heroine central to the action, not a victim but totally responsible for her own destiny.

King Lear is a play, and a tragedy, and can only hint at a longer view; the novel has more scope in that respect, and Emily Brontë is able to reconcile the two views of nature, as both hostile and benign, which both find expression in *Lear* but are left to contradict each other, essentially in opposition. If nature cannot be excluded, and is stronger than culture and civilisation, it follows that nature will, *in time*, redress any balance which has been upset. The natural cycle of the seasons will bring renewal, spring follows on winter, there is birth as well as death. In the second half of the novel Emily Brontë shows us this force at work by reversing the cycle of the first half. The second Catherine is born on the same night that her mother dies, and from then on the whole story is told a second time, in reverse, until a balance between nature and civilisation is achieved.

In the first half of the novel Catherine Earnshaw became Catherine Linton, now Catherine Linton becomes Catherine Earnshaw again. The question of identity in relation to a woman's surname is crucial in *Wuthering Heights*, as it is in *Jane Eyre*: one of Lockwood's first discoveries on sleeping at the Heights are the inscriptions of the first Catherine's name in its various guises, as though she is trying out different identities. The girl who moved from nature to civilisation now moves back: the mother moved from the Heights to Thrushcross Grange, in the second half the daughter moves from the Grange to the Heights. The triangular relationship is played out again, but with different results, results which restore both balance and legitimacy. This time, when Catherine marries Linton, he dies of his own over-civilised degeneracy, leaving her free to marry Hareton Earnshaw. Hareton is natural, he grew up at the Heights and resembles Heathcliff when he was young; but he is also the son of Hindley and therefore the legitimate heir; by marrying him Catherine is not only restored to her natural place but becomes mistress of her childhood home from which the laws of patriarchal inheritance and her brutal brother had excluded her.

The parallels of this reverse cycle are striking. At the beginning of the first cycle Mr Earnshaw went on a journey to Liverpool and came back with the little black savage, the child Heathcliff. At the start of the second cycle Mr Linton, father of the second Catherine, goes on a journey south and comes back with the pale, blonde boy, Linton, as feeble and over-civilised as the other child was wild and strong. As she grows up the younger Catherine longs to explore the forbidden and distant moors, just as her mother, free to roam them, longed for the finery of the Grange. Just as Catherine Earnshaw is 'imprisoned' in the Grange after being attacked by a dog, to come back groomed to be the next Mrs Linton, so Heathcliff imprisons the second Catherine at the Heights and forces her to marry his son.

Heathcliff the man is taking his revenge, but the force of nature is stronger than human nature, and Heathcliff is out-manoeuvred by a nature which juggles with our genes in unforeseen ways. Linton Heathcliff, his own son, has inherited all the worst characteristics of the civilised Linton side, whilst Hareton Earnshaw is more like his aunt Catherine than his weak father. Heathcliff tries to humiliate Hareton, whilst he is forced to recognise that the boy is a reincarnation of himself and Catherine Earnshaw, who are of course one and the same person. This being so, there is nothing left for Heathcliff to do: he dies and joins his other half in the churchyard.

However, the outcome is a reconciliation between nature and civilisation, rather than a clear victory for wild nature which, by itself, is seen as a powerful but destructive force. The second

Catherine has her mother's spirit but is much kinder and more amenable. Hareton, before Catherine Linton gets to work on him, is described in truly Shakespearean terms by Nelly:

> Good things lost amid a wilderness of weeds, to be sure, whose rankness far over-topped their neglected growth; yet, notwithstanding, evidence of a wealthy soil, that might yield luxuriant crops under other and favourable circumstances.[12]

Catherine Earnshaw sets about civilising Hareton when she lives at the Heights. She gives him books, teaches him to read, persuades him to plant flowers in the garden. Heathcliff, recognising Hareton for what he is, with his own youthful spirit and the first Catherine's eyes, finds himself powerless to intervene in this love match, and it is at this time that the ghost of the first Catherine begins to haunt him, calling him to join her. Nelly tells Lockwood that after marriage Hareton and Catherine will move back to the civilised Grange, leaving the primitive Wuthering Heights to old Joseph, the roughest barbarian and unredeemed old savage in the story. The fact that the Linton name has now been wiped out completely seems appropriate: throughout the book one has the feeling that the Linton family do not really 'belong' to the neighbourhood, any more than Lockwood belongs there; the Lintons were civilised intruders from the south, whilst the Earnshaws, as the lintel of Wuthering Heights indicates, have been indigenous to the district for centuries. The name carved on the lintel is 'Hareton Earnshaw', but it is Catherine Linton who teaches him to read it.

Emily Brontë is never sentimental about nature, any more than Shakespeare was. She saw it, as he did, in terms of evolutionary necessity. At fifteen she watched tadpoles in a pond and philosophised on the strong and the weak, and the same philosophy runs through *Wuthering Heights*. Nelly Dean expresses it to Mr Lockwood when she contrasts the behaviour of Edgar Linton and Hindley Earnshaw in similar circumstances of bereavement:

> I used to draw a comparison between him and Hindley Earnshaw and perplex myself to explain satisfactorily why their conduct was so opposite in similar circumstances. They had both been fond husbands, and were both attached to their children; and I could not see how they shouldn't both have taken the same road, for good or

evil. But, I thought in my mind, Hindley, with apparently the
stronger head, has shown himself sadly the worse and the weaker
man . . . they chose their own lots, and were righteously doomed
to endure them. But you'll not want to hear my moralizing,
Mr Lockwood; you'll judge as well as I can, all these things: at
least, you'll think you will, and that's the same.[13]

There is a particular irony in those last words, since Emily Brontë on
the whole leaves her readers to draw their own conclusions; this is one
of the few passages where she does ruminate on the strong and the
weak, and she is clearly doubtful whether some of her readers, the
Mr Lockwoods of the world, will share her vision.

That vision is a unique and daring one, which derives its power
from a vision of cosmic totality embracing the forces of nature,
beautiful but fierce, with moral and existential choice in human
beings. The truth embodied within that vision is really a very simple
one, like, I suspect, all great truths, and it is the force of its simplicity,
reflected in the language, which gives it such imaginative power. It is
a unique achievement in English literature, and as a woman
Catherine Earnshaw remains a unique statement of the female
dilemma and its resolution, though perhaps it is only now that we can
recognise it as such.

9. The Broader View

THE position of women, isolated within individual households, favoured the development of the subjective voice in a fiction which concentrated on the domestic setting. The house remained the central image, though its meaning might change quite radically, and the action tended to be confined to the vicinity of the house and its immediate neighbourhood. The setting was almost always rural, a fact which emphasised women's isolation from modern business and industry. Often they chose to set their story not in contemporary England, but in the past of thirty or forty years ago, as though acknowledging their ignorance of present-day reality. When Charlotte Brontë tried to deal with social themes, to broaden her outlook in *Shirley*, she went back to the Yorkshire of the Napoleonic Wars, and her novel is still essentially rural in character.

But while Charlotte Brontë was writing *Shirley* the wife of a Unitarian minister in Manchester, fresh from a childhood spent in the country, was at last finding time, amongst her many other duties as a mother and helpmate of a social reformer, to put down in fictional form her reaction to the industrial slums of Manchester, and her sympathy for the lives of its inhabitants, whom she tried to help in her position as a minister's wife. Mrs Gaskell was drawn into the realities of the modern world through marriage, but perhaps it was precisely because she was a woman, outside the political and economic power structure, that she was able to open up an entirely new area of human experience with such direct frankness. As a woman she has no particular political axe to grind, nor is she afraid of the consequences of her writing in terms of financial loss or gain, as a 'professional' male writer might have been.

Until the advent of Mrs Gaskell, whose *Mary Barton* appeared in 1848, women novelists had been, for the most part, prevented from social criticism or comment within the novel both by their own exclusion from the world of work and by their own precarious position as women writers which, as we have seen, tended to force them into conservative attitudes both to protect their personal reputations and to ensure them some kind of reading public. Fanny

Burney, in particular, stifled what was at the very least a strong uneasiness about social injustice in order to keep the favour of her royal patrons.

Edgeworth, whose life was in many ways atypical for the women writers of her period, did venture into the realms of social comment. Her experience of estate management in Ireland led her to criticise English absentee landlords in *The Absentee*, where she exposes the abuses to which Irish tenants are reduced when English landlords never come near their estates. And in *Patronage*, published two years later in 1814, she offers a very ambitious analysis of the evils of private patronage in the sphere of politics, as a form of corruption which is bad for individuals and bad for the state. But, like Burney, Edgeworth was nervous of going too far: she hesitated before daring to criticise pressgangs in the novel, and there is nothing in either of the two novels which could offend a Burkean conservative. In *Patronage* the evil and corruption of patronage are contrasted with independence and endeavour, and in *The Absentee* the absentee English landlord is contrasted with the good English landlord who looks after his tenants in a paternalist fashion.

When women did begin to comment on the social system in fiction their outlook was essentially humanist. Leaving aside isolated statements on the position of their own sex, which occur in the writings of all women, from Jane Austen to Mary Wollstonecraft, they tended to stand aside from and, indeed, distrust political systems and solutions and view the problems they described in terms of human relations. In attempting to analyse the breakdown and failure of human relations they tended to blame male behaviour, and see the solution in terms of the feminisation of society.

Though unlike anything written before or since, Mary Shelley's *Frankenstein*, published in 1818, is in fact a critique of destructive masculine values on a social, even global level. Victor Frankenstein and the Arctic explorer who discovers him, tells his story, and is almost his double in temperament, represent male ambition and endeavour which is essentially mechanistic, destructive, and anti-humanist, whilst humanist values are represented by the female characters which their behaviour helps to destroy.

While the Arctic explorer has left behind a sister to follow a deadly and unnatural ambition by going into regions of cold and ice, Victor has left behind his adopted sister and intended bride to create his unnatural monster. Ironically, he is trying to create a human being from corpses, when a wife can create a natural and beautiful human being without dabbling in any black arts, a point which Frankenstein seems to have forgotten entirely in his ill-fated attempt to play God. The fact that there are two sexes, and that they both have a part to play in the world, only comes home to Frankenstein when the nameless monster reads Milton and demands a mate from his creator, an Eve to his Adam. Having ignored this dimension completely, Frankenstein is forced to refuse to create a female monster. Through his disastrous conduct his own 'child' brother is destroyed, then the women in his household, including his bride Elizabeth. And because the monster is Frankenstein's own *alter ego* he is not only to blame, but knows in advance that the monster will destroy the happy domestic scene on which he has turned his back to carry out his experiments in the city.

From the beginning Elizabeth, the beautiful orphaned daughter of highborn parents who fought for the liberty of their country, is interested in poetry and the beauties of nature, while Frankenstein's own interests are scientific and analytical. Humanistic values are also associated with his boyhood friend Clerval, also destroyed by the monster. Clerval is interested in poetry and romance, the beauties of nature, and 'occupied himself . . . with the moral relations of things'. Language, literature, nature, the moral relations of things and politics are associated with humanist values, and on all these the new Prometheus, Frankenstein, turns his back:

> I confess that neither the structure of languages, nor the code of governments, nor the politics of various states possessed attractions for me. It was the secrets of heaven and earth that I desired to learn.[1]

It is on these humanist values, associated with the female character, that Frankenstein turns his back. As his diabolical experiments, which are loathsome and unnatural, progress his enjoyment of life is destroyed:

> my eyes were insensible to the charms of nature . . . . And the same feelings which made me neglect the scenes around me caused me also to forget those friends who were so many miles absent . . . .[2]

Whilst Clerval is a joyous person, 'alive to every new scene' Frankenstein is 'haunted by a curse that shut up every avenue of enjoyment'; he becomes gloomy and despondent:

> I appeared rather like one doomed by slavery to toil in the mines, or any other unwholesome trade than an artist occupied by his favourite employment.

He suffers from fevers and avoids his fellow man. Meanwhile the monster, who begins life in pathetic innocence, himself points the moral when he asks for a mate: 'If I have no ties and no affections, hatred and vice must be my portion.'[3]

The restless and destructive male drive exemplified in the story of Frankenstein and in that of the Arctic explorer who hears his story, learns from it, and turns his ship homeward, has global implications:

> . . . if no man allowed any pursuit whatsoever to interfere with the tranquillity of his domestic affections, Greece had not been enslaved, Caesar would have spared his country, America would have been discovered more gradually, and the empires of Mexico and Peru had not been destroyed.[4]

On his deathbed Frankenstein implores Walton, the explorer, already under pressure from his seamen to give up the perilous voyage, to 'Seek happiness in tranquillity and avoid ambition, even if it be only the apparently innocent one of distinguishing yourself in science and discoveries.'[5]

In *Mary Barton* Elizabeth Gaskell gave her own interpretation of *Frankenstein*, by no means unrelated but translated into political terms of class division, though she seems to be confusing Frankenstein with his creation, who never has a name:

> The actions of the uneducated seem to be typified in those of Frankenstein, that monster of human qualities, ungifted with a soul, a knowledge of the difference between good and evil.
>
> The people rise up to life; they irritate us, they terrify us, and we become their enemies. Then, in the sorrowful moment of our triumphant power, their eyes gaze on us with mute reproach. Why have we made them what they are; a powerful monster, yet without the inner means of peace and happiness?[6]

Throughout *Mary Barton* the conflict between workers and employers is seen as a failure to communicate. Women saw themselves as more able to communicate than men, often as mediators, and it is quite likely that Elizabeth Gaskell felt herself, as a woman, particularly able to speak for the working-class people she knew and understood.

But as a writer Gaskell was unusual in making working-class characters speak for themselves, and in the very first chapter John Barton eloquently speaks of the great divide between rich and poor:

> If I am sick, do they come and nurse me? . . . If I am out of work for weeks in the bad times, and winter comes, with black frost, and keen east wind, and there is no coal for the grate, and no clothes for the bed, and the thin bones are seen through the ragged clothes, does the rich man share his plenty with me, as he ought to do, if his religion were not a humbug? . . . No, I tell you, it's the poor, and the poor only, as does such things for the poor. Don't think to come over me with the old tale, that the rich know nothing of the trials of the poor. I say, if they don't know, they ought to know. We are their slaves as long as we can work; we pile up their fortunes with the sweat of our brows, and yet we live as separate as if we were in two worlds . . .

On the whole Elizabeth Gaskell herself is prepared to give the rich the benefit of the doubt, and assume that they did not really know how the poor suffered. Her own religion, whilst making her a lifelong activist in relieving the distress of the poor, also forbade her to nurse bitter grievances, and John Barton's bitterness is not condoned by the author, though it is certainly understood.

As in Charlotte Brontë's *Shirley*, women are seen as mediators in the bitter divisions between men. The death of John Barton's wife marks a turning point in his life, leading to the murder of the millowner's son:

> One of the good influences over John Barton's life had departed that night. One of the ties which bound him down to the gentle humanities of earth was loosened, and henceforward the neighbours all remarked he was a changed man. His gloom and his sternness became habitual instead of occasional. He was more obstinate.[7]

As in *Frankenstein*, it is women who tie men to 'the gentle humanities of earth'. This is not a new idea: Shakespeare often made women the mediators, Volumnia in *Coriolanus*, Portia in *The Merchant of Venice*, for instance, stand outside the struggle for power and wealth, and are therefore able to represent superior Christian virtues of mercy and forgiveness.

Charlotte Brontë put forward very similar ideas in *Shirley*, published the year after *Mary Barton*. In her novel the millowner Robert Moore is depicted as an obstinate and rigid man, who helps to incite the frame-breakers by his rigid pride and his refusal to communicate with and show sympathy for the people he is putting out of work. Caroline Helstone recognises this destructive trait in his character and tries to change him by a fireside reading of *Coriolanus*, thus herself becoming a female mediator, but the lesson is not taken to heart. After Moore has finished reading *Coriolanus* she tells him:

> . . . you must not be proud to your workpeople; you must not neglect chances of soothing them, and you must not be of an inflexible nature, uttering a request as austerely as if it were a command.[8]

Both Gaskell and Brontë make it clear that they regard employers as just as vulnerable to the vicissitudes of trade as the people they employ, and in both stories there is a recession for which the millowners are in no way to blame. They are to blame for conflict and suffering in so far as they fail to communicate by explaining their own problems, and in failing to understand and alleviate the much more dire and immediate problems faced by the labourer who cannot find work. In *Shirley* it is women, principally Shirley with the help of local spinsters and the clergy, who alleviate the distresses of the unemployed poor, and thus minimise the threat of social disruption and unrest. In *Mary Barton* Gaskell as female mediator addresses the reader, presumed to be middle-class, directly:

> At all times it is a bewildering thing to the poor weaver to see his employer removing from house to house, each one grander than the last, till he ends in building one more magnificent than all, or withdraws his money from the concern, or sells his mill to buy an estate in the country, while all the time the weaver, who thinks he and his fellows are the real makers of wealth, is struggling on for

bread for their children, through the vicissitudes of lowered wages, short hours, fewer hands employed, etc.. . . when he could bear and endure much without complaining, could he also see that his employers were bearing their share; he is bewildered and (to use his own phrase) 'aggravated' to see that all goes on just as usual with the mill-owners . . .[9]

And then, anxious to retain her role of mediator and communicator, and not to be condemned as a radical revolutionary, Gaskell adds rather hastily:

I know this is not really the case; and I know what is the truth in such matters: but what I wish to impress is what the workman feels and thinks.

However, the 'truth in such matters' is left unspoken, the reader's sympathy is heavily engaged on the side of the workers, and Gaskell's anxiety not to appear a political propagandist deceived nobody, except perhaps herself. A modern reader cannot help feeling that she was being somewhat naive when she wrote of the book in 1849:

I can remember now that the prevailing thought in my mind at the time when the tale was silently forming itself and impressing me with the force of reality, was the seeming injustice of the inequalities of fortune. Now, if they appeared unjust to the more fortunate, they must bewilder an ignorant man . . .

But she gives the truth about the balance of the book when she goes on to write:

Round the character of John Barton all the others formed themselves; he was my hero, *the* person with whom all my sympathies went, with whom I tried to identify myself at the time, because I believed from personal observation that such men were not uncommon, and would well reward such sympathy and love as should throw light down upon their groping search after the cause of suffering.[10]

However, the sympathy for John Barton is a lot more self-evident than any light on the causes of suffering – other than the obvious ones.

Both Gaskell and Charlotte Brontë tried to disassociate themselves from any political cause, and they were clearly being naive if they thought they could write as mediators between the classes without becoming involved. Religious beliefs and a sense of their own ignorance and inexperience in the world of politics and commerce must have been inhibiting factors. 'No one can feel more deeply than I how *wicked* it is to do anything to excite class against class' Gaskell wrote late in 1848, trying to defend herself against the critical reception of *Mary Barton* as revolutionary propaganda, ignoring the fact that all the criticism came from one class, her own. But perhaps it was this very naivety, this innocence of the ways of the world, which allowed Gaskell to write with such frankness and reach to the heart of the matter. The same lack of prevarication which allowed her to empathise with John Barton also allowed her to write of prostitution with more frankness than her contemporaries. Whilst Dickens had been reluctant to offend his readers by being too specific about Nancy in *Oliver Twist*, Gaskell is very direct about the miseries of prostitution, and sympathetic about the delusions which lead working-class girls into such a life.

For women writers, social pressure combined with piety and a sense of their own insecurity still made for overt conservatism, even when their fresh vision was essentially revolutionary. It is certainly true that both Brontë and Gaskell felt a deep distrust of all political factions, and both women depicted political agitators as people who exploited the ignorance and suffering of the working class. This is Gaskell on politicians:

> You can fancy, now, the hoards of vengeance in his heart against the employers. For there are never wanting those who either in speech or in print, find it their interest to cherish such feelings in the working classes; who know how and when to rouse the dangerous power at their command; and who use their knowledge with unrelenting purpose to either party.[11]

Whilst in *Shirley* the frame-breakers are incited by agitators from outside the district. As the labourer William Farren puts it:

> Them that reckons to be friends to a lower class than their own fro' political motives is never to be trusted; they always try to make their inferiors tools.[12]

Whilst Shirley exclaims that:

> doubt clutches my inmost heart as to whether men exist clement,
> reasonable and just enough to be intrusted with the task of
> reform.[13]

The operative word in this last quotation is 'men', and it is hardly
surprising that women, totally excluded from politics, without even
the minimal right to vote, should have added a healthy distrust of
political parties and factions to their other criticisms of male activities
embedded in these two novels.

Unlike Charlotte Brontë, Elizabeth Gaskell was a contentedly
married woman with a 'normal' family life, and as a result she is less
obsessed with sex roles imposed by society and, in the case of her
heroine, with the misery of frustrated and unspoken love. She deals
frankly with the temptation of upward mobility through marriage,
when the attentions of Harry Carson, the millowner's son, seem to
promise Mary an escape from a life of poverty and drudgery, and no
less frankly with the life of prostitution which would inevitably follow
on such temptation: the novel begins and ends with Mary's aunt
Esther, who has become a prostitute through the very guileless
naivety which now threatens Mary. When Mary is restrained by
maidenly modesty from telling Clem that she loves him and was
wrong in refusing his proposal of marriage, Gaskell does not question
this sexual convention, whilst *Shirley* is full of bitterness at the need for
women to keep silent, as Caroline Helstone pines away. On the other
hand *Mary Barton* ends up as a heroine who shows great courage and
initiative in trying to save her lover from being hanged for a murder
he did not commit, whilst the female characters in *Shirley* remain
inactive spectators, constantly discussing the boredom and frustration
of their female lives. Even when Shirley and Caroline secretly watch
the attack on Moore's mill, instead of staying safely indoors, they are
unable to do anything but watch events unfold.

In spite of the overt similarity of theme between *Shirley* and *Mary
Barton*, which worried Charlotte Brontë, since the books came out
within a year of each other, in *Shirley* the failure of communication
between workers and employers is much more explicitly blamed on
masculine rigidity, and the novel is much more obviously obsessed
with the chasm between the sexes than with any class warfare. The
men in the novel are consistently portrayed as limited by their very

masculinity; they almost all have an inflated conception of their own importance in the sphere of work, and the one thing that does unite workers and employers is a thoroughly sexist attitude to women. Most of the male characters are portrayed as bad husbands and father-figures, because they do not understand women, patronise them, and regard them as lesser beings who are quite content to cook puddings and sew seams. Marriage is discussed by older men and women in terms of deep pessimism, whilst the young heroines, though obviously doomed to end up married anyhow, discuss their present and future lives in terms of discontent and trepidation.

The conflict and rage which remained at a subconscious, or partly subconscious level in *Jane Eyre*, subsumed in fantasy and story-telling, are raw and in the open here, and Brontë cannot let it alone. The resentment against male Christianity and clergymen which simmered in *Jane Eyre* erupts with full force in *Shirley*, in which pompous, self-important clergymen and ridiculous curates figure so prominently. Mr Helstone, Caroline's uncle and guardian, and himself a man of the Church, typifies the attitudes which run so explicitly through the book:

> Nature never intended Mr Helstone to make a very good husband, especially to a quiet wife. He thought, so long as a woman was silent, nothing ailed her, and she wanted nothing . . .. He made no pretence of comprehending women, or comparing them with men: they were different, probably a very inferior order of existence; a wife could not be her husband's companion, much less his confidant, much less his stay. *His* wife, after a year or two, was of no great importance to him in any shape . . . .[14]

The book is full of silent, suffering women: Caroline Helstone, whose silent misery her uncle fails to understand until actual illness causes him concern, the 'old maids' of the district, who are rescued from traditional ridicule and sanctified, whilst the three curates are savagely cut down to size and consigned to the dust.

The book is full of bigoted, opinionated men. 'Equality – yes, Mr Yorke talked about equality, but at heart he was a proud man.' As for his household: 'Theoretically, they decry partiality; no rights of primogeniture are to be allowed in that house; but Matthew is never to be vexed, never to be opposed . . . . This the younger scions know and feel, and at heart they all rebel against the injustice . . . .' As for his daughter:

Rose is a still, and sometimes a stubborn girl now: her mother wants to make of her such a woman as she is herself – a woman of dark and dreary duties – and Rose has a mind full-set, thick-sown with the germs of ideas her mother never knew. It is agony to her often to have ideas trampled on and repressed. She has never rebelled yet: but if hard-driven, she will rebel one day, and then it will be once for all.[15]

Rose is a child in the novel, which implies that a change is taking place with each generation of women. Caroline and Shirley are themselves different from the older, more conservative women in the book, even if they have not solved the problem of being a woman and can only talk about it. Caroline, the silent sufferer, is herself the daughter of the silent, suffering Mrs Pryor, who escaped from a terrible marriage to become an anonymous governess. Her cousin, the older Hortense Moore, is constantly trying to keep Caroline at her sewing, but Shirley, given freedom and self-determination because she has a private income, gives the quiet Caroline a companion with whom she can discuss the frustration of not having real employment, and the vexed question of marriage with that alien species, men.

When she gets down to courtship, some of the typical Charlotte Brontë patterns reassert themselves, in spite of the attempts at social realism. Robert Moore behaves shamefully in trying to marry Shirley for financial gain, as Rochester married Bertha Mason for money. Like Rochester, the proud man has to be brought low before he is a fit husband. Rochester is crippled and blinded by his vengeful wife, Moore is shot and wounded by vengeful, disaffected workers, and then nursed by a bossy woman who 'turned him in his bed as another woman would have turned a babe in its cradle'. Afterwards he confesses himself 'unmanned', with 'no iron mastery of his sensations now'. When Caroline sees him again he is in much the same state of mind as Jane finds Rochester, depressed: 'the state of my mind is inexpressible – dark, barren, impotent'. It is a state of mind which makes him truly receptive to feminine influence at long last, whereas before he was simply using women, as Rochester used them before his final collapse.

Meanwhile, in the courtship between Shirley Keeldar and Louis Moore we get echoes of both *The Professor* and *Jane Eyre*. It is a tutor – pupil relationship as in *The Professor*, but this time the essay that Shirley writes for her tutor, quoted in full, is not on an immigrant to the New World, but, as befits a feminist book, an alternative version to Milton's first woman. Milton, Shirley tells Caroline, was merely describing his cook. Shirley describes Eva as mother to the Titans. But there is also a partial role-reversal in relation to *Jane Eyre*, since in this love story the woman is the rich heiress and the man is a penniless tutor. However, Charlotte Brontë has not lost her penchant for dominant men, and the independent Shirley becomes irritatingly submissive in love, declares 'I will accept no hand which cannot hold me in check', and refuses another suitor on the ground that he is 'not my master'.

Anne Brontë was just as critical of role-playing between the sexes as her sister. To some extent her reputation has been unfairly over-shadowed by that of her sisters, and her literary development between *Agnes Grey* and *The Tenant of Wildfell Hall* is astonishing. She shares many of Charlotte's attitudes, but is closer to Emily in style: her language is direct and simple, and the structure of *Wildfell Hall* bears a resemblance to *Wuthering Heights* which is not, I suspect, co-incidental.

The spoiling of wilful sons, which is such a dominant theme in the social critique presented in women's fiction, and which Elizabeth Gaskell brought to the surface in her portrait of Harry Carson in *Mary Barton*, is Anne Brontë's central obsession, and she treats the theme with a stark and shocking realism. The collapse and ruin of Branwell Brontë inevitably affected all the Brontë sisters, but while Charlotte tried to suppress a reality which she found shameful, and Emily's general philosophy of life could easily absorb and cope with it, quiet, self-effacing Anne used the experience to give a horrifying and convincing portrait of marriage to a man on the downward path which is only discreetly hinted at in the marriage of Caroline's mother in *Shirley*.

In *Agnes Grey*, based on Anne Brontë's own experience as a governess, she describes a monster of a boy put under her charge, and one who bears a striking resemblance to John Reed in *Jane Eyre*. Tom Bloomfield is idolised by his mother and encouraged by his father and uncle to be a 'man', that is, to behave dreadfully. He bosses everybody, particularly his sisters, maintains that the schoolroom and the books in it belong exclusively to him, uses physical violence against his sisters and the governess narrator, kills and tortures the birds and animals he traps. His father comments smugly that 'it is just what *he* used to do when *he* was a boy', whilst his uncle is far

worse in encouraging the boy's destructive propensity. Mr Robson
not only eggs the boy on in his habit of torturing animals, but
introduces him to drink:

> Though not a positive drunkard, Mr Robson habitually swallowed
> great quantities of wine, and took with great relish an occasional
> glass of brandy and water. He taught his nephew to imitate him in
> this to the utmost of his ability, and to believe that the more wine
> and spirits he could take, and the better he liked them, the more he
> manifested his bold and manly spirit, and rose superior to his
> sisters . . . .[16]

This was to become the dominant theme in *The Tenant of Wildfell Hall*,
in which Helen Huntingdon finally escapes from her doomed
marriage to a drunkard and libertine to save her son from the same
fate. In a remarkable account of a deteriorating marriage told by
Helen herself in her diary, we see her concern shift from the marriage
itself, and her own fading hopes of happiness, to concern for the
development of her son. Her own steady influence on the boy is
constantly undermined by her husband, who indulges the boy and
uses him to get at the mother. But the break comes when the father
and his male cronies try to get the boy to follow their example:

> My greatest source of uneasiness, in this time of trial, was my son,
> whom his father and his father's friends delighted to encourage in
> all the embryo vices a little child can show, and to instruct in all the
> evil habits he could acquire – in a word, to 'make a man of
> him' . . . .[17]

The child is taught to:

> tipple wine like papa, to swear like Mr Hattersley, and to have his
> own way like a man, and sent mamma to the devil when she tried
> to prevent him.

The Tenant of Wildfell Hall is a very convincing, as well as terrifying,
portrait of a marriage to a man who is a feckless drunkard and
womaniser with a certain amount of deceptive charm. Anne Brontë
sees Huntingdon's behaviour as the direct consequence of his social
position: he is a man of means with no inner resources and too much

time on his hands, since he does not need to earn a living. This, combined with the parental over-indulgence which was to be the ruin of John Reed, who killed himself after dissipating the family fortune, is seen as the heart of the problem and Helen Huntingdon's main concern is to stop her son being just such a man. Very soon after her marriage she writes:

> I wish he had something to do, some useful trade, or profession, or employment – anything to occupy his head or his hands for a few hours a day, and give him something besides his own pleasure to think about . . . and he has no more idea of exerting himself to overcome obstacles than he has of restraining his natural appetites; and these two things are the ruin of him. I lay them both to the charge of his harsh yet careless father and his madly indulgent mother. If ever I am a mother I will zealously strive against this *crime* of over-indulgence – I can hardly give it a milder name when I think of the evils it brings.[18]

Helen Huntingdon, like Caroline Helstone's mother, willingly chooses the risks attendant on any woman who takes such a course, and leaves her husband. Helen, through bitter personal experience, becomes an independent woman who stands outside society to preserve her self-respect and protect her son. She knows she is flouting the world's opinion and even that of her friends in leaving her husband, and as a tenant of Wildfell Hall she becomes the victim of idle and malicious local gossip. Very early on, as the mysterious Mrs Graham, she argues passionately against women being 'tenderly and delicately nutured, like a hothouse plant – taught to cling to others for direction and support, and guarded, as much as possible, from the very knowledge of evil'.[19] She rounds on her interlocutor in contrasting the sheltered upbringing of girls, whilst boys are exposed to the vices exemplified in the novel:

> You would have us encourage our sons to prove all things by their own experience, while our daughters must not even profit by the experience of others.

Forced by public reaction on to the defensive, Anne Brontë returned to this theme in the preface to the second edition. We have to imagine

ourselves in her social and historical position, the young daughter of a provincial clergyman in Victorian England, to appreciate the bravery of her stand:

> I wished to tell the truth, for truth always conveys its own moral to those who are able to receive it . . . if there were less of this delicate concealment of facts – this whispering 'Peace, peace,' when there is no peace, there would be less of sin and misery to the young of both sexes who are left to wring their bitter knowledge from experience . . . when I feel it my duty to speak an unpalatable truth, with the help of God, I *will* speak it, though it be to the prejudice of my name and to the detriment of my reader's immediate pleasure as well as my own.

Like Charlotte, Anne, although a believing Christian, also found fault with the male religious establishment, and both her novels are critical of clergymen on much the same grounds as the criticisms in *Shirley*. The rector in *Agnes Grey*, in contrast to the sympathetic young clergyman the heroine marries, is portrayed as a social snob, a pulpit exhibitionist with no time or sympathy to spare for his poorer parishioners:

> His favourite subjects were Church discipline, rites and ceremonies, apostolic succession, the duty of reverence and obedience to the clergy, the atrocious criminality of dissent, the absolute necessity of observing all the forms of godliness, the reprehensible presumption of individuals who attempted to think for themselves in matters connected with religion . . . and occasionally (to please his wealthy parishioners) the necessity of deferential obedience from the poor to the rich . . . .[20]

The Church and clergymen figure less prominently in *Wildfell Hall*, but Anne Brontë nevertheless feels strongly enough on the subject to describe the local clergyman as:

> a man of fixed principles, strong prejudices, and regular habits, – intolerant of dissent in any shape, acting under a firm conviction that his opinions were always right, and whoever differed from them, must be, either deplorably ignorant, or wilfully blind.[21]

These portraits have a lot in common with Charlotte Brontë's description of Mr Helstone as 'a man almost without sympathy, ungentle, prejudiced, and rigid' and Shirley's diatribe against the dreadful curates:

> . . . when I hear the outbreak of their silly narrow jealousies and assumptions . . . when I behold their insolent carriage to the poor, their often base servility to the rich, I think the Establishment is indeed in a poor way, and both she and her sons appear in the utmost need of reformation . . .[22]

Such statements, in turn, relate to the clergymen in *Jane Eyre*, who are consistently described as 'rigid', who align themselves with the social establishment, a hierarchy which is male-dominated and excludes both women and the poor. Given such feelings, such bitter resentment and contempt, it is hardly surprising that Charlotte Brontë was at first so averse to marriage with a Puseyite clergyman.

Because of their constricted lives, women as social commentators tended to confine themselves to topics about which they knew most, themes on which they had first-hand experience. The range might be narrower, but treatment could gain through the intensity of first-hand experience. With Branwell Brontë in the house it could hardly be said that the Brontës led a very sheltered life, and life was always a hard struggle at Haworth. Nor were they ever remote from the life of the ordinary people of the district, their language, gossip and feuds. Elizabeth Gaskell also wrote from first-hand experience, once she began to work as a minister's wife in the slums of Manchester. Outside the political system themselves, they tended to see social problems in human and humanitarian terms, to regard male-dominated society as in need of tempering by female influence. Although it might open them to the charge of political naivety it was also their strength: as story-tellers they were less likely to theorise, to use characters merely as examples to prove a point. They identified and sympathised with their characters, instead of patronising or descending to caricature. Their very political innocence allowed them to shock and scandalise a readership anxious to have its views and social position endorsed rather than challenged. As for their view of masculine and feminine influence in the social sphere – history has yet to prove them wrong.

Footnotes

The place of publication is London unless otherwise stated.

INTRODUCTION

1. See W. Gérin's *Charlotte Brontë* for the interesting and revealing notes made inside the front cover of an exercise book in 1843. It was to be written in the first person, set in rural England of thirty to fifty years ago, with a limited number of characters, the plot to be 'domestic', with 'the romantic note excluded'. Her last resolution – 'No grumbling allowed' – was certainly not adhered to.

2. Letter dated 12 July 1872, from *The George Sand – Gustave Flaubert Letters* (Chicago: Academy Chicago Ltd, 1979)

1. BACKGROUND FOR CHANGE

1. Quoted by Lawrence Stone, *The Family, Sex and Marriage in England 1500–1800* (Harmondsworth: Penguin, 1979) pp. 228–33.
2. Ibid.
3. Samuel Richardson, *Sir Charles Grandison*, vol. 1, Letter 13.
4. Henry Fielding, *Joseph Andrews*, book 3, ch. 4.
5. For these figures, and much other background information, see Stone, *The Family, Sex and Marriage* pp. 241–5.
6. Richardson, *Grandison*, vol. 2, Letter 2.
7. Quoted by Stone, *The Family, Sex and Marriage*. p. 242.

2. FINDING A STRUCTURE

1. Richardson, *Grandison*, vol. 1, Letter 8.
2. Dr Samuel Johnson, *The Rambler* (31 March 1750).
3. Maria Edgeworth, *Ormond*, ch. 7.
4. Ibid, ch. 8.
5. Jane Austen, *Northanger Abbey*, ch. 6.
6. Richardson, *Grandison*, vol. 1, Letter 12.
7. Ibid, vol. 1, Letter 18.
8. Austen, *Love and Freindship*.
9. Richardson, *Grandison*, vol. 2, Letter 2.
10. Ibid, vol. 3, Letter 17.

3. ANXIOUS APPOLOGIES

1. Quoted by Stone, *The Family, Sex and Marriage*, etc.
2. Austen, *Sanditon*, ch. 6, pp. 189–90.
3. J. Hemlow (ed.) *Fanny Burney: Journals and Letters*, vol. 3, Letter to Dr Burney, (18 June 1795).
4. Ibid, vol. 3, Windsor Journal (6 July 1796).
5. Ibid, vol. 1, Letter to her sister (October 1791).
6. Quoted by Marilyn Butler, *Maria Edgeworth: A Literary Biography* (Oxford: O.U.P., 1972).
7. Ibid.
8. Hannah More, *Cœlebs in Search of a Wife*, ch. 18.
9. Edgeworth, *Belinda*, vol. 3, ch. 30.
10. Edgeworth, *Leonora*, Letter 2.
11. Ibid, Letter 1.
12. Ibid, Letter 6.
13. Ibid, Letter 11.
14. Ibid, Letter 44.
15. Austen, *Northanger Abbey*, ch. 5.
16. R. W. Chapman (ed.), *Jane Austen: Letters*, vol. 1 (18 December 1778).
17. 'Biographical Notice of Ellis and Acton Bell' from the 1850 edition of *Wuthering Heights*.

4. FANNY BURNEY

1. Burney, *Evelina*, vol. 2, Letter 8.
2. Ibid.
3. Ibid. vol. 2, Letter 2.
4. Ibid, vol. 2, Letter 19.
5. Ibid, vol. 2, Letter 15.
6. Ibid, vol. 2, Letter 21.
7. Burney, *The Wanderer*, Dedication 'To Doctor Burney'.
8. Ibid.
9. Burney, *Journals and Letters*, vol. 2 (February 1793).
10. Quoted in the dedication of *The Wanderer*.
11. Burney, *Cecilia*, book 3, ch. 7.
12. Ibid, book 7, ch. 1.
13. Burney, *Journals and Letters*, vol. 2 (31 May 1793).
14. Ibid (9 June 1793).
15. Ibid, vol. 3.
16. Ibid, vol. 3.
17. Ibid, vol. 3.
18. Ibid, vol. 3.
19. Burney, *Camilla*, book 5, ch. 5.

20. Ibid, book 4, ch. 8.
21. *Evelina*, vol. 2, Letter 30.
22. Burney, *The Wanderer*, vol. 2, book 4, ch. 29.
23. Ibid, vol. 2, book 3, ch. 22.
24. Ibid, vol. 2, book 3, ch. 28.
25. Ibid, vol. 2, book 4, ch. 36.

5. THE GOTHIC ALTERNATIVE

1. Mary Wollstonecraft, writing anonymously in the *Analytical Review*, July 1788, criticised *Emmeline* for its lack of realism, which was likely to have a bad influence on readers: 'The false expectations these wild scenes excite, tend to debauch the mind, and throw an insipid kind of uniformity over the moderate and rational prospects of life.'

2. Wollstonecraft, *Mary*, ch. 24.

3. Ibid, ch. 18.

4. Ibid, ch. 1.

5. 'I have just been reading, for the fourth time, I believe, *The Simple Story*, which I intended this time to read as a critic, that I might write to Mrs. Inchbald about it: but I was so carried away by it that I was totally incapable of thinking of Mrs. Inchbald or anything but Miss Milner and Doriforth, who appeared to me real persons whom I saw and heard, and who had such power to interest me, that I cried my eyes out before I came to the end of the story: I think it is the most pathetic and the most powerfully interesting tale I ever read.' (Letter to Miss Ruxton, December 1809) *Maria Edgeworth: Chosen Letters*, ed. F. V. Barry (Cape, 1931) p. 213.

6. Inchbald, *A Simple Story*, vol. 1, ch. 4.

7. Ibid, vol. 4, ch. 10.

8. Smith: *Emmeline*, vol. 1, ch. 1.

9. Ibid, vol. 1, ch. 5.

10. Ibid, ch. 15.

11. Ibid, ch. 12.

12. Ibid, vol. 2, ch. 1.

13. Ibid, vol. 4, ch. 8.

14. Ibid, vol. 3, ch. 4.

15. Ibid, vol. 4, ch. 11.

16. 'That the highest degree of reverence should be paid to youth, and that nothing indecent should be suffered to approach their eyes or ears; are precepts extorted by sense and virtue from an ancient writer, by no means eminent for chastity of thought. The same kind, tho' not the same degree of caution, is required in every thing which is laid before them, to secure them from unjust prejudices, perverse opinions, and incongruous combinations of images.

In the romances formerly written, every transaction and sentiment was so remote from all that passes among men, that the reader was in very little danger of making any applications to himself . . . .. But when an adventurer is levelled with the rest of the world, and acts in such scenes of the universal drama, as may be the lot of any other man; young spectators fix their eyes upon him with closer attention, and hope by observing his behaviour and success to regulate their own practices . . . . But if the power of example is so great . . . care ought to be taken that . . . the best examples only should be exhibited . . .' Dr Samuel Johnson, *The Rambler* (31 March 1750).

17. Mrs Radcliffe, *The Mysteries of Udolpho*, vol. 1, ch. 1.

18. Ibid, vol. 1, ch. 1.

19. Ibid, ch. 7.

20. Ibid, ch. 10.

21. Ibid, ch. 19.

22. Wollstonecraft, *Maria* or *The Wrongs of Woman*, ch. 3.

6. THE SUPREMACY OF SENSE

1. Quoted by J. E. Austen, *A Memoir of Jane Austen*.

2. Letter to Cassandra Austen, 14 June 1814, from *Jane Austen's Letters*, ed. R. W. Chapman.

3. Ibid, To Cassandra, 27 October 1798.

4. Ibid, To Fanny Knight, 18 November 1814.

5. Ibid.

6. *The Journals and Letters of Fanny Burney* edited by J. Hemlow *et al.* Letter to Mrs Waddington, 19 September 1793.

7. Austen, *Northanger Abbey*, ch. 24 (or vol. 2, ch. 9).

8. Ibid, ch. 25 (or vol. 2, ch. 10).

9. Ibid, ch. 29 (or vol. 2, ch. 14).

10. Edgeworth, *Belinda*, vol. 1, ch. 3.

11. Ibid.

12. Ibid, vol. 1, ch. 16.

13. Ibid, vol. 2, ch. 19.

14. Ibid.

15. West, *A Gossip's Story*, vol. 1, ch. 1.

16. Ibid, vol. 1, ch. 4.

17. Ibid, vol. 1, ch. 10.

18. Ibid, vol. 1, ch. 16.

19. Austen, *Sense and Sensibility*, vol. 1, ch. 10.

20. West, *A Gossip's Story*, vol. 2, ch. 35.

21. Ibid, vol. 1, ch. 35.

22. Hannah More, *Cœlebs in Search of a Wife*, Preface.

23. Ibid, ch. 39. In Chapter 2 Cœlebs' mother had made similar comments on choosing a wife:

The education of the present race of females is not very favourable to domestic happiness. For my part I call education, not that which smothers a woman with accomplishments, but that which tends to consolidate a firm and regular system of character; that which tends to form a friend, a companion, and a wife. I call education, not that which is made up of the shreds and patches of useless arts, but that which inculcates principles, polishes taste, regulates temper, cultivates reason, subdues the passions, directs the feelings, habituates to reflection, trains to self-denial, and, more especially, that which refers all actions, feelings, sentiments, tastes, and passions, to the love and fear of God.

24. Ibid, ch. 23.

25. Ibid, ch. 2.

26. Ibid, ch. 14.

27. Austen, *Sense and Sensibility*, ch. 50 (or vol. 3, ch. 14).

28. Austen was herself aware of the problem. She wrote to Cassandra on 29 January 1813: 'The work is rather too light, and bright, and sparkling; it wants shade; it wants to be stretched out here and there with a long chapter of sense, if it could be had.'

29. Austen, *Pride and Prejudice*, ch. 41 (or vol. 2, ch. 18).

30. Ibid, ch. 60 (or vol. 3, ch. 13).

31. Ibid, ch. 61 (or vol. 3, ch. 14).

32. Ibid, ch. 22 (or vol. 1, ch. 22).

33. Ibid, ch. 42 (or vol. 2, ch. 19).

34. Austen, *Mansfield Park*, ch. 48 (vol. 3, ch. 17).

35. Richardson, *Grandison*, vol. 4, Letter 24.

36. 'A Collection of Letters' from *Love and Freindship and Other Early Works* (Women's Press Ltd, 1978).

37. Austen, *Mansfield Park*, ch. 20, (or vol. 2, ch. 2).

38. Ibid, ch. 21 (or vol. 2, ch. 2).

39. Ibid, ch. 18 (vol. 1, ch. 18).

40. Ibid, ch. 9 (vol. 1, ch. 9).

41. Ibid, ch. 17 (vol. 1, ch. 17).

42. Austen, *Emma*, ch. 10 (vol. 1, ch. 10).

43. Austen, *Sense and Sensibility*, ch. 46 (vol. 3, ch. 10).

44. Austen, *Emma*, ch. 46 (vol. 3, ch. 10).

45. Ibid, ch. 20 (vol. 2, ch. 2).

46. Letter to Anna Austen, 9 September 1814.

47. Austen, *Persuasion*, ch. 4 (vol. 1, ch. 4).

48. Ibid, ch. 4.

49. Ibid, ch. 1.

50. Ibid, ch. 10.

51. Ibid, ch. 10.

52. Ibid, ch. 11.

53. 'Biographical Notice of The Author' which prefaced the posthumous first edition of *Persuasion* in 1818.

7. THE SUPPRESSED SELF

1. Martineau, *Deerbrook*, ch. 15.
2. Austen, *Northanger Abbey*, ch. 1.
3. Martineau, *Deerbrook*, ch. 21.
4. Letter to G. H. Lewes, 12 January 1848, quoted by E. Gaskell, *The Life of Charlotte Brontë*.
5. Ibid, Letter to G. H. Lewes, 6 November 1847.
6. See W. Gérin, *Charlotte Brontë*.
7. Gérin, General Introduction, *Five Novelettes* (Folio Press, 1971). Also quoted in Gilbert & Gubar, *The Madwoman in the Attic* (Yale U.P., 1979).
8. C. Brontë, *The Professor*, ch. 12.
9. Ibid, ch. 17.
10. Ibid, ch. 18.
11. C. Brontë, *Shirley*, ch. 24.
12. Ibid, ch. 19.
13. Ibid, ch. 19.
14. Ibid, ch. 20.
15. C. Brontë, *Jane Eyre*, ch. 1.
16. Ibid, ch. 2.
17. Ibid, ch. 2.
18. Ibid, ch. 3.
19. Ibid, ch. 2.
20. Ibid, ch. 3.
21. Ibid, ch. 4.
22. Ibid, ch. 6.
23. Ibid, ch. 7.
24. S. Freud, 'Female Sexuality' (1931).
25. C. Brontë, *Jane Eyre*, ch. 7.
26. Ibid, ch. 9.
27. Ibid, ch. 10.
28. Ibid, ch. 11.
29. Ibid, ch. 12.
30. Ibid, ch. 14.
31. Ibid, ch. 15.
32. Ibid.
33. Ibid, ch. 16.
34. Ibid, ch. 19.
35. Ibid, ch. 24.
36. Ibid, ch. 25.

37. Ibid, ch. 27.
38. Ibid, ch. 34.
39. Ibid, ch. 36.
40. Letter of 6 November 1847.

8. WUTHERING HEIGHTS

1. C. Brontë, *Shirley*, ch. 12.
2. Quoted by W. Gérin, *Emily Brontë*.
3. C. Brontë, *Shirley*, ch. 12.
4. E. Brontë, *Wuthering Heights*, ch. 18.
5. Ibid, ch. 3.
6. Ibid, ch. 9.
7. Ibid, ch. 10.
8. Ibid, ch. 9.
9. Ibid, ch. 15.
10. Ibid, ch. 8.
11. Ibid, ch. 12.
12. Ibid, ch. 18.
13. Ibid, ch. 17.

9. THE BROADER VIEW

1. M. Shelley, *Frankenstein*, ch. 2.
2. Ibid, ch. 4.
3. Ibid, ch. 17.
4. Ibid, ch. 4.
5. Ibid, ch. 24.
6. E. Gaskell, *Mary Barton*, ch. 15.
7. Ibid, ch. 3.
8. C. Brontë, *Shirley*, ch. 6.
9. E. Gaskell, *Mary Barton*, ch. 3.
10. Quoted by W. Gérin, *Elizabeth Gaskell*.
11. *Mary Barton*, ch. 3.
12. C. Brontë, *Shirley*, ch. 18.
13. Ibid, ch. 21.
14. Ibid, ch. 4.
15. Ibid, ch. 9.
16. A. Brontë, *Agnes Grey*, ch. 5.
17. A. Brontë, *The Tenant of Wildfell Hall*, ch. 39.
18. Ibid, ch. 25.
19. Ibid, ch. 3.
20. A. Brontë, *Agnes Grey*, ch. 10.
21. A. Brontë, *The Tenant of Wildfell Hall*, ch. 1.
22. C. Brontë, *Shirley*, ch. 21.

Select Bibliography

JANE AUSTEN

J. Austen, *Lady Susan, The Watsons, Sanditon* (Harmondsworth: Penguin, 1974).

————, *Letters to her sister Cassandra & others,* collected and edited by R. W. Chapman (Oxford: Oxford University Press, 1932, repr. 1952).

————, *Novels,* edited by R. W. Chapman, (Oxford: Oxford University Press, 1926, repr. 1952).

M. Butler, *Jane Austen and The War of Ideas* (Oxford: Oxford University Press, 1975).

ANNE BRONTË

A. Brontë, *The Tenant of Wildfell Hall* (Harmondsworth: Penguin, 1979).

W. Gérin, *Anne Brontë* (Nelson, 1959).

CHARLOTTE BRONTË

C. Brontë, *'The Professor' and 'Emma'* (Everyman, Dent, 1969).

E. Gaskell, *The Life of Charlotte Brontë* (Harmondsworth: Penguin, 1975).

W. Gérin, *Charlotte Brontë, The Evolution of Genius* (Oxford: Oxford University Press, 1967).

Clement K. Shorter, *Charlotte Brontë and her Circle* (Hodder & Stoughton, 1896, repr. as *The Brontës and Their Circle*, Dent, 1914).

EMILY BRONTË

W. Gérin, *Emily Brontë* (Oxford: Oxford University Press, 1971).

FANNY BURNEY

F. Burney, *Camilla* (Oxford: Oxford University Press, 1972).

————, *Evelina* (Oxford: Oxford University Press, 1970).

————, *Journals and Letters* vols 1–8 edited by Joyce Hemlow and others, (Oxford: Oxford University Press, 1972–80).

MARIA EDGEWORTH

M. Butler, *Maria Edgeworth* (Oxford: Oxford University Press, 1972).

M. Edgeworth, *Castle Rackrent* (Oxford: Oxford University Press, 1964).

—————, *Chosen Letters*, introduced by F. V. Barry, (Cape, 1931).

ELIZABETH GASKELL
E. Gaskell, *The Letters of Mrs Gaskell*, edited by J. A. V. Chapple and A. Pollard, (Manchester: Manchester University Press, 1966).

ELIZABETH INCHBALD
E. Inchbald, *A Simple Story* (Oxford: Oxford University Press, 1967).

HARRIET MARTINEAU
V. Wheatley, *Life and Work of Harriet Martineau* (Secker & Warburg, 1957).

ANN RADCLIFFE
A. Radcliffe, *The Mysteries of Udolpho* (Oxford: Oxford University Press, 1980).

CHARLOTTE SMITH
C. Smith, *Emmeline, The Orphan of the Castle* (1971).

MARY WOLLSTONECRAFT
M. Wollstonecraft, *'Mary' and 'The Wrongs of Woman'* (Oxford: Oxford University Press, 1976).

GENERAL BACKGROUND READING
Ellen Moers, *Literary Women* (The Women's Press, 1978).
Virginia Woolf, *Women and Writing* (The Women's Press, 1978).

Index